Ruby on Rails Development

Rapid Web Application Creation with the Rails Framework

Greyson Chesterfield

COPYRIGHT

DISCLAIMER

The information provided in this book is for general informational purposes only. All content in this book reflects the author's views and is based on their research, knowledge, and experiences. The author and publisher make no representations or warranties of any kind concerning the completeness, accuracy, reliability, suitability, or availability of the information contained herein.

This book is not intended to be a substitute for professional advice, diagnosis, or treatment. Readers should seek professional advice for any specific concerns or conditions. The author and publisher disclaim any liability or responsibility for any direct, indirect, incidental, or consequential loss or damage arising from the use of the information contained in this book.

Contents

Introduction

The world of web development is constantly evolving, with new frameworks, tools, and technologies emerging to address the growing demands for speed, efficiency, and scalability. Among these, **Ruby on Rails** has remained a cornerstone for developers seeking to create robust web applications quickly and effectively. With its philosophy of "Convention over Configuration" and "Don't Repeat Yourself (DRY)," Rails empowers developers to focus on building features rather than wasting time on repetitive tasks or boilerplate code.

This book, **"Rapid Web Application Creation with the Rails Framework,"** is designed to guide readers through the exciting journey of mastering Ruby on Rails, from absolute beginners to seasoned developers. Whether you're stepping into the world of web development for the first time or looking to deepen your understanding of Rails, this book provides a comprehensive roadmap to help you build modern web applications efficiently.

Why Ruby on Rails?

Ruby on Rails, often simply called Rails, is an open-source web application framework written in the Ruby programming language. Launched in 2004 by

David Heinemeier Hansson, Rails introduced a paradigm shift in web development, making rapid application development a reality. Rails provides developers with pre-built structures for handling common web development tasks, such as database integration, routing, and user authentication, so they can focus on the unique aspects of their applications.

Rails has been the framework behind some of the most successful web platforms, including **GitHub, Shopify, Basecamp, and Airbnb.** These success stories demonstrate that Rails is not only suitable for prototyping and small projects but also scalable for large, high-traffic applications.

Who Is This Book For?

This book is crafted with a diverse audience in mind:

- **Beginners**: If you're new to programming or web development, this book will introduce you to the fundamental concepts of Rails in a way that's easy to follow. You'll learn by building real projects, which will give you hands-on experience as you go.

- **Intermediate Developers**: If you already have some experience with programming or other web frameworks, this book will help you transition into the Rails ecosystem, teaching you best practices and advanced features that can enhance your productivity.

- **Professionals and Hobbyists**: For those looking to streamline their web development workflows or explore Rails as a tool for side projects, this book offers actionable insights, real-world examples, and practical tips that you can immediately apply to your work.

What Makes Rails Unique?

There are countless web frameworks available today, but Rails continues to stand out due to its developer-friendly features:

1. **Convention Over Configuration**: Rails comes with sensible defaults, reducing the need for configuration. This allows developers to start building right away without getting bogged down in setup details.

2. **Full-Stack Framework**: Rails includes everything you need to build a complete web application, from handling front-end templates to back-end database management.

3. **Strong Ecosystem**: With its rich library of gems (plugins) and active community, Rails makes it easy to add functionality to your application without reinventing the wheel.

4. **Focus on Productivity**: Rails emphasizes rapid development, allowing developers to achieve more in less time, making it an ideal choice for startups and agile teams.

What You'll Learn in This Book

This book is structured to take you step-by-step through the process of building web applications with Rails. Each chapter builds on the last, ensuring that you develop a solid understanding of both fundamental concepts and advanced techniques. Here's a brief overview of what you'll gain:

- **Core Concepts**: Learn the Rails philosophy, how it implements the MVC (Model-View-Controller) pattern, and how its conventions speed up development.

- **Practical Skills**: Build hands-on projects like blogs, e-commerce platforms, and RESTful APIs, giving you real-world experience.

- **Advanced Features**: Explore topics like authentication, authorization, testing, background jobs, and scaling to ensure your applications are production-ready.

- **Best Practices**: Understand how to write clean, maintainable code, optimize performance, and follow security best practices.

- **Real-World Applications**: Discover how to implement features that are essential in modern web development, such as real-time updates, API integrations, and localization.

Why Focus on Rapid Development?

In today's fast-paced world, speed is everything. Businesses need to launch applications quickly to stay competitive, and developers must adapt to meet these demands. Rails is uniquely suited to this challenge, allowing teams to move from idea to deployment in record time. However, rapid development doesn't mean compromising on quality. Throughout this book, you'll learn how to maintain a balance between speed and robustness, ensuring that your applications are both fast to build and reliable in production.

How This Book Is Structured

This book is divided into chapters that follow a logical progression, starting with the basics and gradually introducing more complex topics. Each chapter includes:

1. **Conceptual Explanations**: Clear, jargon-free explanations of key concepts.

2. **Step-by-Step Tutorials**: Guided exercises that walk you through building specific features.

3. **Hands-On Projects**: Practical examples that reinforce your learning and provide a portfolio of real-world applications.

4. **Challenges and Solutions**: Opportunities to test your skills with coding challenges, followed by detailed solutions to help you learn from your mistakes.

5. **Best Practices**: Tips and insights to help you write clean, efficient, and maintainable code.

How to Get the Most Out of This Book

To maximize your learning experience, consider the following tips:

- **Practice Actively**: Don't just read the code examples—type them out and experiment with them. Modify the examples to see how they work and apply the concepts to your own projects.

- **Ask Questions**: As you progress, you may encounter concepts that are challenging. Take the time to research, experiment, and ask for help when needed.

- **Build Your Portfolio**: Use the projects in this book as a starting point to build your own applications. Having a portfolio of completed projects is invaluable for showcasing your skills.

- **Engage with the Community**: The Rails community is one of its greatest strengths. Join forums, contribute to open-source projects, and connect with other developers to enhance your learning.

Final Thoughts

The goal of this book is not just to teach you Ruby on Rails but to empower you as a developer. By the end of this journey, you'll have the skills and confidence to build web applications from scratch, tackle real-world challenges, and stay competitive in the ever-changing world of web development. Whether you're building a personal project, contributing to an open-source initiative, or launching the next big startup, Rails will be an invaluable tool in your toolkit.

So, let's dive in and start creating something amazing with Rails. Together, we'll explore the art of rapid web application development and unlock the potential of one of the most powerful frameworks available today.

Chapter 1: Introduction to Ruby on Rails

Understanding Rails and Its Ecosystem

Ruby on Rails, often simply referred to as "Rails," is a powerful web application framework written in the Ruby programming language. Since its inception in 2004, Rails has revolutionized web development by simplifying the process of building complex applications and emphasizing developer productivity. Its design philosophy centers on making programming enjoyable while maintaining high standards for code quality and maintainability.

At its core, Rails is built around the **Model-View-Controller (MVC)** architectural pattern. This design separates application logic into three distinct components:

- **Model**: Handles data, database interactions, and business logic.

- **View**: Responsible for the presentation layer and user interface.

- **Controller**: Manages the communication between models and views, processing user inputs and triggering the appropriate application actions.

This separation ensures that Rails applications are modular, maintainable, and scalable. Developers can easily update one part of the application without affecting others, which is essential for growing projects.

Rails is not just a framework; it's part of a larger ecosystem that includes a variety of tools, libraries, and community resources. For instance:

- **Gems**: RubyGems, Rails' package manager, provides access to thousands of reusable code libraries (gems) that extend the functionality of Rails applications.

- **Active Record**: The ORM (Object-Relational Mapping) system in Rails simplifies database interactions by representing database records as Ruby objects.

- **Action View**: The layer that handles templating and rendering views for user interfaces.

- **Rails Command-Line Interface (CLI)**: Offers powerful tools to generate boilerplate code, run migrations, and manage applications efficiently.

The Rails community is a vibrant and active part of the ecosystem. With forums, conferences, and an abundance of tutorials and documentation, developers of all skill levels can find support and resources to solve problems and learn new techniques.

The Philosophy of "Convention Over Configuration"

One of the defining features of Rails is its adherence to the philosophy of **"Convention over Configuration" (CoC).** This principle eliminates the need for developers to make numerous decisions about minor details when starting a new project. Instead, Rails assumes a set of sensible defaults, allowing developers to focus on building functionality rather than configuring every aspect of their application.

Here's how CoC manifests in Rails:

1. **Standardized File Structure**: Rails applications follow a predictable directory structure. Models are stored in the app/models directory, views in app/views, and controllers in app/controllers. This organization ensures that any developer

familiar with Rails can easily navigate and understand a new project.

2. **Implicit Naming Conventions**: Rails uses intuitive naming conventions to link components. For example, a database table named users is automatically mapped to a User model, and the controller responsible for handling user-related actions is named UsersController. Developers don't need to write additional configuration to establish these relationships.

3. **Default Behaviors**: Many tasks in Rails come with built-in defaults. For instance, when you scaffold a new resource, Rails generates code for creating, reading, updating, and deleting records (CRUD operations) without requiring explicit setup.

By adopting CoC, Rails reduces cognitive load and accelerates development. Developers can rely on Rails' conventions to handle common patterns and edge cases, while still retaining the flexibility to override defaults when necessary.

What Makes Rails Ideal for Rapid Development?

Ruby on Rails has earned its reputation as a framework for **rapid application development (RAD)**. Startups, small teams, and even large enterprises turn to Rails to deliver web applications efficiently without sacrificing quality. Several features make Rails uniquely suited for this purpose:

---

1. Scaffolding and Code Generation

Rails includes a powerful command-line tool that allows developers to generate boilerplate code in seconds. Scaffolding, for instance, creates a fully functional resource with minimal effort. By running a single command, Rails generates:

- A model for database interactions.

- A controller for managing application logic.

- Views for displaying data to users.

- Routes for connecting URLs to the appropriate actions.

This automated approach significantly reduces the time required to set up a new feature, allowing developers to focus on customizing and refining their application.

2. Built-in Tools for Common Tasks

Rails provides integrated solutions for many of the repetitive tasks developers encounter during web development. For example:

- **Active Record** simplifies database operations with methods like find, save, and update. Developers can write concise, readable code to query and manipulate data.

- **Action Mailer** allows for easy integration of email functionality, making it simple to send notifications, confirmations, or other automated messages.

- **Asset Pipeline** streamlines the management of JavaScript, CSS, and other static files, ensuring efficient loading and versioning.

These tools save countless hours that would otherwise be spent writing custom implementations.

3. Emphasis on DRY (Don't Repeat Yourself)

Rails encourages developers to follow the DRY principle, which aims to minimize code duplication. By leveraging reusable components, helpers, and modules, developers can write clean and maintainable code that reduces redundancy. For example:

- Shared logic can be abstracted into concerns or modules, making it accessible across multiple parts of the application.

- View templates can utilize partials to render reusable UI components, like headers or forms.

This focus on reusability not only speeds up development but also makes it easier to maintain and extend applications over time.

---

4. Integrated Testing Framework

Rails places a strong emphasis on test-driven development (TDD) and includes testing tools out of the box. Features like fixtures, test helpers, and assertions make it easy to write comprehensive tests for models, controllers, and views. By encouraging testing from the start, Rails ensures that applications are robust and less prone to errors as they grow.

---

5. Strong Community and Ecosystem

The Rails community is one of its greatest assets. With an active network of contributors, Rails evolves rapidly to incorporate the latest trends and technologies. Developers benefit from:

- Thousands of open-source gems that add functionality to Rails applications.

- A wealth of online tutorials, forums, and guides for troubleshooting and learning.

- Regular updates and security patches that keep Rails applications modern and secure.

This collaborative ecosystem ensures that developers have the support and resources needed to build applications efficiently.

6. Ruby Language Features

Rails inherits many of its strengths from Ruby, the language it is built on. Ruby's syntax is clean, expressive, and intuitive, making it a joy to work with. Features like blocks, mixins, and metaprogramming give developers powerful tools to write concise and flexible code. Ruby's focus on developer happiness aligns perfectly with Rails' goal of making web development enjoyable.

7. Deployment Readiness

Rails simplifies the deployment process, offering tools and best practices for launching applications quickly. Popular hosting platforms like Heroku and AWS provide pre-configured environments optimized for Rails, further reducing setup time. Features like database migrations ensure that changes to the application can be deployed seamlessly, even in live environments.

8. Scalability and Performance

Although Rails is often associated with rapid prototyping, it is equally capable of supporting large-scale, high-performance applications. Techniques such as caching, database optimization, and background jobs enable Rails to handle high traffic and complex business logic. Many large companies, including Shopify and GitHub, rely on Rails to power their platforms.

Ruby on Rails has transformed the landscape of web development by emphasizing simplicity, productivity, and scalability. Its ecosystem, rooted in conventions and best practices, empowers developers to create powerful applications with minimal effort. By adopting principles like "Convention over Configuration" and "Don't Repeat Yourself," Rails eliminates unnecessary complexity and allows developers to focus on what matters most: building great software.

In the chapters ahead, we will explore how to harness the power of Rails to create web applications that are not only quick to develop but also robust, maintainable, and scalable. Whether you're building your first application or refining your skills as a seasoned developer, Rails offers the tools and philosophy to turn your ideas into reality.

Chapter 2: Setting Up Your Development Environment

To harness the power of Ruby on Rails and begin building web applications, the first step is to set up a development environment that suits your needs. This chapter will guide you through the essential steps of installing Ruby and Rails on various platforms, configuring a text editor or integrated development environment (IDE), and understanding the fundamentals of version control with Git. A well-prepared environment ensures a smooth development process and minimizes common setup issues.

Installing Ruby and Rails on Different Platforms

Ruby on Rails is cross-platform, meaning it can be installed on macOS, Windows, and Linux. Each operating system has its nuances, and this section covers the step-by-step process for setting up Rails on your chosen platform.

1. macOS

macOS is a popular choice for Rails development due to its Unix-based architecture, which is similar to most production environments.

1. **Install Homebrew**
   Homebrew is a package manager for macOS that simplifies software installation.
   Run this command in the terminal to install Homebrew:

bash

```
/bin/bash -c "$(curl -fsSL https://raw.githubusercontent.com/Homebrew/install/HEAD/install.sh)"
```

2. **Install Ruby**
   Use Homebrew to install Ruby:

bash

```
brew install ruby
```

Verify the installation by checking the Ruby version:

bash

```
ruby -v
```

3. **Install Node.js and Yarn**
   Rails requires a JavaScript runtime. Install
   Node.js and Yarn via Homebrew:

bash

brew install node

brew install yarn

4. **Install Rails**
   Use the gem command to install Rails:

bash

gem install rails

Confirm the installation by checking the Rails
version:

bash

rails -v

2. Windows

Rails development on Windows has historically
been more challenging, but modern tools like

Windows Subsystem for Linux (WSL) have made it significantly easier.

1. **Install WSL**
   Enable WSL to create a Linux-like environment within Windows. Follow Microsoft's instructions to install WSL and set up a Linux distribution (e.g., Ubuntu).

2. **Install Ruby**
   Inside WSL, use a Ruby version manager like rbenv or rvm:

bash

```
sudo apt update

sudo apt install rbenv

rbenv install 3.2.0

rbenv global 3.2.0
```

3. **Install Rails**
   Use gem to install Rails within WSL:

bash

```
gem install rails
```

4. **Alternative: RailsInstaller**
   For simpler setups, use RailsInstaller

(https://railsinstaller.org/). However, this method is less flexible than WSL.

---

3. Linux

Linux is ideal for Rails development, offering flexibility and performance similar to production environments.

1. **Update Your System**
   Run the following commands to update your system:

bash

```
sudo apt update

sudo apt upgrade
```

2. **Install Ruby**
   Use a version manager like rvm or rbenv:

bash

```
sudo apt install rbenv

rbenv install 3.2.0

rbenv global 3.2.0
```

3. **Install Dependencies**
   Rails requires additional libraries:

bash

sudo apt install nodejs yarn

4. **Install Rails**
   Use gem to install Rails:

bash

gem install rails

5. **Verify Installation**
   Confirm that both Ruby and Rails are installed:

bash

ruby -v

rails -v

Configuring a Text Editor or IDE

Choosing the right text editor or IDE can significantly impact your productivity and comfort while coding. Here are some popular options for Rails development:

---

1. Visual Studio Code (VS Code)

VS Code is a lightweight and versatile text editor with extensive plugin support.

- **Installation**: Download from Visual Studio Code.

- **Essential Extensions**:

    o Ruby (syntax highlighting and snippets)

    o Rails Go To Spec (quickly navigate to test files)

    o ERB Formatter (for formatting Rails views)

    o GitLens (for enhanced Git integration)

- **Configuration**: Create a workspace and customize settings via settings.json to tailor the editor to your workflow.

---

2. JetBrains RubyMine

RubyMine is a professional IDE specifically designed for Ruby and Rails development.

- **Features**:

  - Built-in Rails support for views, models, and controllers.

  - Advanced debugging and refactoring tools.

  - Integrated testing frameworks.

- **Setup**: Download RubyMine from JetBrains. Use the free trial or subscribe for full access.

3. Sublime Text

Sublime Text is another popular choice for its speed and simplicity.

- **Installation**: Download from Sublime Text.

- **Key Plugins**:

  - Ruby on Rails snippets.

  - GitGutter (displays Git changes in the editor).

  - SideBarEnhancements (improves file navigation).

4. Vim/NeoVim

For developers comfortable with terminal-based

tools, Vim or NeoVim offers unparalleled speed and configurability.

- **Setup**:

  - ○ Install plugins like vim-rails, vim-ruby, and ctrlp for Rails development.

  - ○ Customize the .vimrc file to add shortcuts and enable syntax highlighting.

Introducing Version Control with Git

Version control is essential for managing changes in your codebase, collaborating with team members, and ensuring that your work is always recoverable. Git is the most widely used version control system, and understanding its basics is crucial for Rails development.

1. Installing Git

Git is available for all major operating systems.

- **macOS**: Git comes pre-installed. If not, install it via Homebrew:

bash

brew install git

- **Windows**: Download Git for Windows from git-scm.com.

- **Linux**: Use your package manager:

bash

sudo apt install git

Verify the installation:

bash

git --version

---

2. Basic Git Commands

Here are some fundamental Git commands that every developer should know:

- **Initialize a Repository**: Create a new Git repository in your project directory.

```bash
git init
```

- **Check Status**: View the status of your repository.

```bash
git status
```

- **Stage Changes**: Add changes to the staging area.

```bash
git add .
```

- **Commit Changes**: Save changes to the repository.

```bash
git commit -m "Commit message"
```

- **View History**: Check the commit history.

bash

git log

---

3. Remote Repositories

Git works seamlessly with remote repositories hosted on platforms like GitHub, GitLab, and Bitbucket.

- **Clone a Repository**: Download an existing repository.

bash

git clone <repository_url>

- **Push Changes**: Upload your commits to the remote repository.

bash

git push origin main

- **Pull Changes**: Download updates from the remote repository.

bash

git pull origin main

---

4. Best Practices for Version Control

- **Commit Often**: Break your work into small, manageable chunks and commit frequently.

- **Write Descriptive Commit Messages**: Summarize the changes clearly.

- **Use Branches**: Create separate branches for new features or bug fixes to keep the main branch stable.

bash

git checkout -b feature_branch

- **Collaborate with Pull Requests**: Use pull requests to review and merge code collaboratively.

---

5. Git and Rails Workflow

In Rails projects, Git is invaluable for tracking changes in models, controllers, views, and configurations. A typical workflow might look like this:

1. Initialize a Git repository in your Rails project:

bash

```
git init
```

2. Create a .gitignore file to exclude unnecessary files:

bash

```
/log

/tmp

.DS_Store

node_modules
```

3. Commit your changes regularly and push to a remote repository for backup and collaboration.

Setting up your development environment is the foundation of any successful Rails project. By following the steps outlined in this chapter, you'll have a fully functional environment tailored to your platform, equipped with tools to maximize productivity, and backed by version control to manage your codebase effectively.

Whether you're on macOS, Windows, or Linux, the process of installing Ruby and Rails is straightforward, and configuring your preferred text editor or IDE ensures a comfortable coding experience. With Git as your version control system, you'll have the tools to track changes, collaborate with others, and safeguard your work as you embark on your Rails development journey.

Chapter 3: Rails Architecture and the MVC Pattern

Ruby on Rails is often celebrated for its adherence to the **Model-View-Controller (MVC)** architecture. This chapter delves deep into the MVC pattern, explores how Rails implements it, and illustrates its utility with real-world examples. By the end of this chapter, you'll understand the role of each component, how they interact in a Rails application, and how to leverage this architecture to build scalable and maintainable web applications.

Understanding the Model-View-Controller Pattern

The **Model-View-Controller (MVC)** pattern is a software design paradigm that separates an application's concerns into three interconnected components:

1. **Model**
   The model represents the application's data, business logic, and rules. It interacts with the database and ensures that the application

state is consistent and accurate.
Key responsibilities:

- Defining the structure of data through classes.

- Validating inputs and maintaining data integrity.

- Implementing business rules and domain logic.

2. **View**

The view is responsible for the presentation layer. It generates the user interface based on the data provided by the model and the instructions from the controller.
Key responsibilities:

- Displaying data to the user in a readable and interactive format.

- Responding to user inputs visually (e.g., through buttons or forms).

3. **Controller**

The controller acts as the intermediary between the model and the view. It processes user inputs, communicates with the model, and decides which view to render.
Key responsibilities:

- Receiving user input from HTTP requests.

- Fetching or modifying data via the model.

- Rendering views based on the application's state or user actions.

Benefits of the MVC Pattern

The MVC architecture offers several advantages that make it ideal for web application development:

- **Separation of Concerns**: By dividing the application into three distinct layers, developers can work on models, views, or controllers independently without affecting the other layers.

- **Maintainability**: Changes in one component (e.g., the view) are less likely to impact other parts of the application, making it easier to update and extend.

- **Testability**: Testing is simplified because each component has a specific role, allowing developers to write focused unit tests.

- **Scalability**: The modular nature of MVC supports large and complex applications by keeping the codebase organized and manageable.

How Rails Implements MVC

Rails is built around the MVC pattern, and its conventions make it intuitive to follow this architecture. Let's examine how Rails handles each component:

1. Models in Rails

Models in Rails are Ruby classes that interact with the database through **Active Record**, the Object-Relational Mapping (ORM) library included in Rails. Active Record simplifies database interactions by representing tables as Ruby objects and rows as instances of these objects.

Example: Defining a User model

ruby

```
class User < ApplicationRecord
  validates :name, presence: true
  validates :email, presence: true, uniqueness: true
end
```

Key features of Rails models:

- **Data Validation**: Ensures the integrity of user inputs (e.g., validates :email, presence: true).

- **Associations**: Defines relationships between models (e.g., has_many :posts).

- **Query Methods**: Provides methods like find, where, and order to retrieve data from the database.

Example: Fetching users from the database

ruby

```
@users = User.where(active: true).order(:created_at)
```

---

2. Views in Rails

Rails views are responsible for rendering the user interface using Embedded Ruby (ERB) templates. These templates combine HTML and Ruby code to display dynamic content.

Example: Rendering a list of users

erb

```
<% @users.each do |user| %>

 <p><%= user.name %> - <%= user.email %></p>

<% end %>
```

Key features of Rails views:

- **Layouts and Partials**: Views can include reusable components (partials) and layouts for consistent page structure.

- **Helper Methods**: Rails provides helper methods to simplify common tasks like formatting dates or creating links.

Example: Using a helper method

erb

```
<%= link_to "Edit", edit_user_path(user) %>
```

3. Controllers in Rails

Controllers in Rails handle incoming HTTP requests, process user inputs, and interact with the model and view to generate a response. They are the backbone of user interaction.

Example: A UsersController with basic CRUD actions

ruby

```ruby
class UsersController < ApplicationController
  def index
    @users = User.all
  end

  def show
    @user = User.find(params[:id])
  end

  def new
    @user = User.new
  end

  def create
    @user = User.new(user_params)
    if @user.save
      redirect_to @user
    else
```

```
  render :new

 end

end


 private


 def user_params

  params.require(:user).permit(:name, :email)

 end

end
```

Key features of Rails controllers:

- **Routing Integration**: Controllers map directly to routes, as defined in the config/routes.rb file.

- **Strong Parameters**: Ensures secure handling of form inputs.

- **Redirects and Renders**: Controls the flow of the application by redirecting to other actions or rendering views.

Real-World MVC Examples in Rails

To understand how the MVC pattern works in practice, let's consider a real-world example: a blog application.

Example: Blog Application

1. **Model**
   Define a Post model to represent blog posts:

ruby

```
class Post < ApplicationRecord

  validates :title, presence: true

  validates :content, presence: true

end
```

2. **Controller**
   Create a PostsController to manage blog posts:

ruby

```
class PostsController < ApplicationController

  def index

    @posts = Post.all
```

```ruby
  end


  def show
    @post = Post.find(params[:id])
  end


  def new
    @post = Post.new
  end


  def create
    @post = Post.new(post_params)
    if @post.save
      redirect_to @post
    else
      render :new
    end
  end


  private
```

```ruby
def post_params
  params.require(:post).permit(:title, :content)
end
end
```

3. **View**
   Create an ERB template to display posts:

erb

```erb
<h1><%= @post.title %></h1>
<p><%= @post.content %></p>
```

4. **Routes**
   Define routes in config/routes.rb:

ruby

```ruby
resources :posts
```

Example: E-Commerce Application

In an e-commerce platform, MVC components might include:

- **Model**: Product, Order, and Customer classes to manage data.

- **View**: Templates for displaying product listings and order summaries.

- **Controller**: ProductsController and OrdersController to handle user interactions like adding items to a cart.

Common Challenges with MVC in Rails

While the MVC pattern is powerful, developers often encounter challenges when implementing it:

1. **Overloaded Controllers**
   Controllers can become bloated with too much logic. To address this, Rails encourages extracting logic into services or concerns.

2. **Complex Views**
   Views with extensive logic can become difficult to maintain. Use helpers or presenters to simplify view templates.

3. **Tight Coupling**
   Over-reliance on Rails conventions can lead to tightly coupled code. Following the Single Responsibility Principle and modular design helps mitigate this.

Rails' implementation of the MVC pattern is one of its most defining and powerful features. By separating concerns into models, views, and controllers, Rails ensures that applications are organized, maintainable, and scalable. Each component has a clear role, and their interactions enable seamless development workflows.

In this chapter, you've learned the theory behind MVC, how Rails adopts it, and its practical application in real-world scenarios. Understanding this architecture is essential for building robust Rails applications and lays the groundwork for exploring advanced features in subsequent chapters.

Chapter 4: Creating Your First Rails Application

Building a web application from scratch can seem like a daunting task, but Ruby on Rails simplifies this process with its developer-friendly tools and conventions. This chapter will guide you step-by-step through creating your first Rails application, explain the framework's file structure, and teach you how to run and test your application using the Rails server. By the end, you'll have a functional web application and a strong understanding of the foundational elements of Rails.

Setting the Stage: What You'll Build

For this tutorial, we'll create a simple web application called **"BlogApp"**—a platform where users can create, read, update, and delete (CRUD) blog posts. This small but powerful project will help you understand how Rails components work together and lay the groundwork for more complex applications.

Scaffolding a Basic Web App

Rails provides a powerful tool called **scaffolding** that automates the generation of boilerplate code for a fully functional web resource. With a single command, Rails generates models, views, controllers, routes, and database migrations. Let's start building the BlogApp.

Step 1: Creating a New Rails Application

Begin by creating a new Rails application with the following command:

bash

```
rails new BlogApp
```

This command does several things:

1. Creates a new directory named BlogApp.

2. Initializes the Rails framework inside the directory.

3. Sets up a default file structure for the application.

4. Installs necessary dependencies, such as gems and the database.

Move into your project directory:

bash

cd BlogApp

Step 2: Generating a Scaffold for Blog Posts

Use the **scaffold generator** to create resources for managing blog posts:

bash

rails generate scaffold Post title:string content:text

Here's what this command does:

- **Model**: Creates a Post model with attributes title (string) and content (text).

- **Database Migration**: Generates a migration file to create a posts table in the database.

- **Controller**: Generates a PostsController with standard CRUD actions (index, show, new, edit, create, update, destroy).

- **Views**: Creates ERB templates for each CRUD action.

- **Routes**: Updates the config/routes.rb file to define RESTful routes for posts.

Step 3: Migrating the Database

Rails migrations are used to manage changes to the database schema. Run the following command to apply the generated migration and create the posts table:

bash

```
rails db:migrate
```

This command:

1. Reads the migration file in db/migrate/.

2. Executes SQL commands to create the database table.

3. Updates the database schema to reflect these changes.

Step 4: Running the Rails Server

Start the Rails development server:

bash

```
rails server
```

By default, the server runs on http://localhost:3000. Open this URL in your browser, and you'll see the default Rails welcome page.

To access your blog post resource, navigate to:

bash

http://localhost:3000/posts

Congratulations! You've just created a fully functional web resource for managing blog posts.

File Structure Overview

Rails applications follow a standardized file structure that organizes the various components of the framework. Understanding this structure is crucial for navigating and modifying your application.

Root Directory

When you generate a Rails application, the root directory contains several important files and folders:

1. **app/**
   This is the core of your application. It

contains subdirectories for models, views, controllers, and other application logic.

2. **config/**
   Contains configuration files for your application, including routes (routes.rb), database settings, and initializers.

3. **db/**
   Stores database-related files, including migrations and the schema.

4. **public/**
   Contains static files such as images and HTML files.

5. **Gemfile**
   Specifies the gems (libraries) your application depends on.

Inside the app/ Directory

The app/ directory is where most of your application logic resides. Let's break down its subdirectories:

1. **models/**
   Contains Ruby classes that represent the data and business logic of your application. Each model corresponds to a database table.

Example: app/models/post.rb

ruby

```
class Post < ApplicationRecord
  validates :title, presence: true
  validates :content, presence: true
end
```

2. **views/**
   Contains templates for rendering the user interface. Templates are written in Embedded Ruby (ERB) or other supported templating languages.

Example: app/views/posts/index.html.erb

erb

```
<h1>All Posts</h1>
<% @posts.each do |post| %>
  <p><%= post.title %></p>
<% end %>
```

3. **controllers/**
   Contains the application logic that connects models and views. Each controller

corresponds to a resource and includes actions like index, show, create, etc.

Example: app/controllers/posts_controller.rb

ruby

```ruby
class PostsController < ApplicationController
 def index
  @posts = Post.all
 end
end
```

4. **helpers/**
   Contains helper modules for views. These are used to extract complex logic from templates.

5. **assets/**
   Stores front-end assets like CSS, JavaScript, and images.

Other Key Directories

1. **config/routes.rb**
   Defines the URL structure of your application. For example:

ruby

resources :posts

2. **db/**
   Contains migration files and the schema, which define the structure of your database.

Example:
db/migrate/20220101000000_create_posts.rb

ruby

```ruby
class CreatePosts < ActiveRecord::Migration[6.1]
  def change
    create_table :posts do |t|
      t.string :title
      t.text :content
      t.timestamps
    end
  end
end
```

Running the Rails Server

Running the Rails server is a critical part of the development process. Here's how you can make the most of this tool.

Starting the Server

Use the following command to start the Rails development server:

bash

```
rails server
```

By default, the server listens on port 3000. You can specify a different port if needed:

bash

```
rails server -p 4000
```

Debugging with the Server Logs

While the server is running, Rails outputs log messages to the terminal. These logs provide valuable insights, such as:

- HTTP requests and responses.

- Errors and exceptions.

- Database queries.

Stopping the Server

To stop the server, press Ctrl+C in the terminal.

Enhancing Your Web App

Once your application is running, you can start customizing it by adding features and refining the design. For example:

1. **Styling**: Use CSS or integrate a framework like Bootstrap for a polished look.

2. **Forms**: Create forms to allow users to input data, such as new blog posts.

3. **Validation**: Add model validations to ensure data integrity.

In this chapter, you've taken your first steps into the world of Rails by creating a functional web application from scratch. You've learned how to use Rails' scaffolding to generate resources, explored the framework's file structure, and successfully ran the Rails server to view your application in action.

With this foundational knowledge, you're ready to dive deeper into Rails and begin customizing your application to meet more complex requirements. Building on this simple blog example, you'll soon be able to create dynamic, feature-rich applications that bring your ideas to life.

Chapter 5: Routes and URL Handling

In a Ruby on Rails application, routes are the first point of interaction between a user's browser and your application. They determine how HTTP requests are directed to specific controllers and actions. Understanding how to configure routes, leverage RESTful routing, and create custom routes is essential for building dynamic, well-structured Rails applications. This chapter explores the intricacies of Rails routing, explaining how it works and providing practical examples.

Introduction to Rails Routing

In Rails, routing is managed by the **config/routes.rb** file. This file defines the rules that map HTTP requests to controller actions. When a user visits a URL, Rails checks the routes file to find the corresponding action to execute.

For example, a basic route might look like this:

ruby

```
get '/welcome', to: 'pages#welcome'
```

This route maps an HTTP GET request to /welcome to the welcome action in the PagesController.

Configuring Routes in Rails

The Rails router provides a powerful DSL (Domain-Specific Language) for defining routes. Here are the core components you'll work with:

1. Basic Routes

The simplest way to define a route is to specify the HTTP method, URL pattern, and controller action:

ruby

```
get '/about', to: 'pages#about'
```

- **HTTP Method**: Specifies the type of request (e.g., GET, POST, PUT, DELETE).

- **URL Pattern**: Defines the path users visit (e.g., /about).

- **Controller and Action**: Indicates the controller (pages) and action (about) to execute.

2. Root Route

The root route determines the default page of your application (e.g., the homepage). To set a root route, use:

ruby

```
root 'pages#home'
```

This maps the root URL (/) to the home action in the PagesController.

---

3. Dynamic Segments

Dynamic segments allow routes to capture variables from the URL. These variables are passed to the controller as parameters.

Example:

ruby

```
get '/posts/:id', to: 'posts#show'
```

If a user visits /posts/5, the id parameter will be set to 5 in the show action of the PostsController.

Accessing the parameter in the controller:

ruby

```ruby
class PostsController < ApplicationController
  def show
    @post = Post.find(params[:id])
  end
end
```

4. Named Routes

Named routes simplify URL generation by providing a shorthand name for a route. Use the as option to define a named route:

ruby

```ruby
get '/contact', to: 'pages#contact', as: 'contact'
```

You can now use the route helper in your views or controllers:

erb

```erb
<%= link_to 'Contact Us', contact_path %>
```

Understanding RESTful Routing

Rails embraces the principles of **REST (Representational State Transfer)**, a standard architectural style for designing APIs and web applications. RESTful routing is a core concept in Rails, providing a consistent and intuitive way to map HTTP requests to CRUD (Create, Read, Update, Delete) operations.

1. Resources and RESTful Routes

The resources method in Rails automatically generates a set of RESTful routes for a given resource. For example:

ruby

```
resources :posts
```

This single line generates the following routes:

HTTP Method	Path	Controller#Action	Purpose
GET	/posts	posts#index	List all posts
GET	/posts/:id	posts#show	View a specific post
GET	/posts/new	posts#new	Display new

			post form
POST	/posts	posts#create	Create a new post
GET	/posts/:id/edit	posts#edit	Display edit form
PATCH/PUT	/posts/:id	posts#update	Update a post
DELETE	/posts/:id	posts#destroy	Delete a post

2. Customizing RESTful Routes

You can customize RESTful routes to fit specific needs. For example, if your application doesn't require all actions, use the only or except options:

ruby

resources :posts, only: [:index, :show]

resources :comments, except: [:destroy]

You can also add custom routes within a resource block:

ruby

```ruby
resources :posts do

  member do

    get 'preview'

  end


  collection do

    get 'archived'

  end

end
```

- **Member Routes**: Operate on a single resource (e.g., /posts/:id/preview).
- **Collection Routes**: Operate on the entire collection (e.g., /posts/archived).

---

3. Nested Resources

Nested resources represent relationships between models. For example, if a post has many comments, you can nest the comments resource under posts:

ruby

```ruby
resources :posts do

  resources :comments

end
```

This generates routes like:

- /posts/:post_id/comments (index)

- /posts/:post_id/comments/:id (show)

In the CommentsController, you can access the parent post_id:

ruby

```ruby
class CommentsController < ApplicationController

  def index

    @post = Post.find(params[:post_id])

    @comments = @post.comments

  end

end
```

Creating Custom Routes

While RESTful routing covers most use cases, custom routes allow you to handle unique requirements.

1. Non-RESTful Routes

Custom routes are useful for actions that don't fit the standard CRUD operations. For example:

ruby

```
get '/dashboard', to: 'users#dashboard'
```

2. Route Constraints

You can add constraints to routes to limit them to specific formats, subdomains, or patterns.

Example: Restricting a route to JSON requests:

ruby

```
get '/api/posts', to: 'posts#api', constraints: { format: 'json' }
```

Example: Subdomain-based routing:

ruby

```
constraints subdomain: 'admin' do
  namespace :admin do
```

```ruby
  resources :dashboard

 end

end
```

---

3. Redirects

Routes can also perform redirects:

ruby

```ruby
get '/old_path', to: redirect('/new_path')
```

---

4. Custom Route Matchers

The match method provides more flexibility for defining routes:

ruby

```ruby
match '/about', to: 'pages#about', via: :all
```

The via option specifies the allowed HTTP methods (:get, :post, :put, etc.).

---

5. Namespace and Scope

Namespaces group controllers under a common module, often used for admin sections or APIs.

Example:

ruby

```
namespace :admin do

  resources :posts

end
```

This creates routes like /admin/posts and maps them to Admin::PostsController.

Scopes allow additional flexibility, such as adding prefixes or constraints:

ruby

```
scope '/api' do

  resources :posts

end
```

Advanced Topics in Routing

1. Routing Concerns

Concerns allow you to define reusable routing patterns. For example:

ruby

```
concern :commentable do

  resources :comments

end


resources :posts, concerns: :commentable

resources :photos, concerns: :commentable
```

2. Rails Path Helpers

Rails automatically generates helper methods for routes. For example:

- posts_path → /posts

- new_post_path → /posts/new

- edit_post_path(@post) → /posts/:id/edit

These helpers simplify URL generation in views and controllers.

Best Practices for Routing

1. **Keep Routes RESTful**: Favor RESTful conventions whenever possible to maintain clarity and consistency.

2. **Use Descriptive Names**: Ensure route names clearly describe their purpose (e.g., archived_posts_path).

3. **Avoid Deep Nesting**: Limit nested routes to one level to prevent complexity and maintain readability.

4. **Group Related Routes**: Use namespaces and scopes to organize related routes logically.

5. **Test Routes**: Use Rails' route testing features to verify that your routes behave as expected.

Routing is the backbone of any Rails application, bridging the gap between user requests and your application's logic. By mastering Rails' routing system, you can create clean, intuitive, and efficient routes that form the foundation of a well-organized application.

In this chapter, you've learned:

1. How to configure basic and dynamic routes in Rails.

2. The principles of RESTful routing and how to customize them.

3. Techniques for creating custom routes, including nested resources, constraints, and namespaces.

By leveraging these routing capabilities, you'll be equipped to design robust and scalable web applications with Rails.

Chapter 6: Active Record Basics

In the Ruby on Rails ecosystem, **Active Record** serves as the Object-Relational Mapping (ORM) library, bridging the gap between your Ruby application and its database. By leveraging Active Record, you can interact with database tables as if they were Ruby objects, streamlining the development process and reducing boilerplate code. This chapter delves into the basics of Active Record, including its ORM features, how to generate and migrate databases, and performing CRUD (Create, Read, Update, Delete) operations.

Introduction to Object-Relational Mapping (ORM)

Object-Relational Mapping (ORM) is a design pattern that connects an object-oriented programming language with a relational database. It abstracts the complexities of SQL queries, allowing developers to interact with database records using objects and methods in their preferred language.

For example, instead of writing raw SQL like:

sql

```sql
SELECT * FROM users WHERE id = 1;
```

With Active Record, you can simply write:

ruby

```ruby
User.find(1)
```

This abstraction makes your code cleaner, more maintainable, and less error-prone.

Benefits of ORM in Rails

1. **Simplified Database Interactions**: ORM reduces the need to write raw SQL, replacing it with intuitive Ruby methods.

2. **Database-Agnostic Code**: Active Record works with various database systems (e.g., SQLite, PostgreSQL, MySQL) without requiring significant code changes.

3. **Data Validation and Integrity**: Active Record provides built-in validation methods to ensure data integrity.

4. **Seamless Relationships**: It simplifies working with related tables through associations like has_many and belongs_to.

Active Record, as Rails' default ORM, follows the **Active Record Pattern**, where each database table is represented by a corresponding Ruby class.

Generating and Migrating Databases

Before you can interact with a database, you need to define its structure. Active Record provides tools to generate database tables and manage their schema through migrations.

1. Generating a Model

In Rails, models are Ruby classes that correspond to database tables. Generating a model automatically creates:

- A model file in app/models/.

- A migration file in db/migrate/.

Command:

bash

rails generate model User name:string email:string

This command:

1. Creates a User model in app/models/user.rb:

ruby

```ruby
class User < ApplicationRecord
end
```

2. Generates a migration file in db/migrate/:

ruby

```ruby
class CreateUsers < ActiveRecord::Migration[6.1]
  def change
    create_table :users do |t|
      t.string :name
      t.string :email
      t.timestamps
    end
  end
end
```

---

2. Understanding Migrations

Migrations are Ruby files that describe changes to the database schema. They are used to:

- Create, modify, or delete tables.

- Add or remove columns.

- Add indexes or constraints.

Example: Adding a new column to the users table

bash

rails generate migration AddAgeToUsers age:integer

Generated migration:

ruby

```ruby
class AddAgeToUsers <
ActiveRecord::Migration[6.1]
  def change
    add_column :users, :age, :integer
  end
end
```

3. Running Migrations

To apply migrations and update the database schema, run:

bash

rails db:migrate

Rails maintains a migration history in the schema_migrations table to ensure that migrations are only applied once.

---

4. Rolling Back Migrations

If you need to undo a migration, use:

bash

rails db:rollback

This is particularly useful during development when testing changes to the schema.

---

5. Schema File

After running migrations, Rails generates a db/schema.rb file, which represents the current structure of the database. This file is used to track changes and provide a snapshot of the database schema.

Performing CRUD Operations with Active Record

CRUD (Create, Read, Update, Delete) operations are the foundation of any web application. Active Record makes these operations simple and intuitive by mapping them to Ruby methods.

---

1. Create

To create a new record, you can use the new method followed by save, or the create method.

Example: Creating a user

ruby

```
# Using new and save
user = User.new(name: "Alice", email: "alice@example.com")

user.save


# Using create
user = User.create(name: "Bob", email: "bob@example.com")
```

Active Record automatically generates the SQL to insert the record into the database.

---

2. Read

Active Record provides several methods to retrieve data from the database:

- **Find by ID:**

ruby

```
user = User.find(1)
```

- **Find All:**

ruby

```
users = User.all
```

- **Query with Conditions:**

ruby

```
users = User.where(age: 25)
```

- **First and Last Records:**

ruby

```ruby
first_user = User.first
```

```ruby
last_user = User.last
```

- **Order and Limit:**

ruby

```ruby
users = User.order(:name).limit(5)
```

---

3. Update

To update an existing record, retrieve it, modify its attributes, and save the changes.

Example: Updating a user

ruby

```ruby
user = User.find(1)
user.name = "Updated Name"
user.save
```

Alternatively, use the update method:

ruby

```ruby
user.update(name: "Updated Name")
```

4. Delete

To delete a record, use the destroy method:

ruby

```
user = User.find(1)
user.destroy
```

Alternatively, delete multiple records:

ruby

```
User.where(age: 25).destroy_all
```

Active Record Validations

Validations ensure that only valid data is saved to the database. You define validations in the model.

Example: Adding validations to the User model

ruby

```
class User < ApplicationRecord
```

```ruby
validates :name, presence: true
validates :email, presence: true, uniqueness: true
end
```

- presence: Ensures a field is not empty.
- uniqueness: Ensures a field is unique.
- length: Validates the length of a field.
- format: Validates the format using a regex.

Example: Custom validation

ruby

```ruby
class User < ApplicationRecord
  validate :email_domain_check

  private

  def email_domain_check
    unless email.ends_with?("@example.com")
      errors.add(:email, "must be from the example.com domain")
    end
```

end

end

Active Record Associations

Associations define relationships between models. Common types include:

1. **One-to-Many**:

ruby

```
class User < ApplicationRecord
  has_many :posts
end


class Post < ApplicationRecord
  belongs_to :user
end
```

2. **Many-to-Many**:

ruby

```
class Post < ApplicationRecord
```

```
  has_and_belongs_to_many :tags
end


class Tag < ApplicationRecord
 has_and_belongs_to_many :posts
end
```

3. **One-to-One**:

ruby

```
class User < ApplicationRecord
 has_one :profile
end


class Profile < ApplicationRecord
 belongs_to :user
end
```

Associations allow you to query related data seamlessly:

ruby

```
user = User.find(1)

posts = user.posts
```

Active Record Callbacks

Callbacks allow you to hook into the lifecycle of a model object. Common callbacks include:

- before_save: Executes before saving the record.

- after_create: Executes after creating a record.

Example:

ruby

```
class User < ApplicationRecord
  before_save :normalize_name


  private


  def normalize_name
    self.name = name.downcase.titleize
  end
```

end

Advanced Topics

1. Scopes

Scopes allow you to define reusable queries in your model:

ruby

```
class User < ApplicationRecord
  scope :active, -> { where(active: true) }
end


users = User.active
```

---

2. Eager Loading

Eager loading minimizes database queries when fetching associated records:

ruby

```
users = User.includes(:posts).all
```

Active Record simplifies database interactions, enabling you to focus on building features rather than managing SQL. In this chapter, you've learned how to:

1. Use Active Record's ORM features to map database tables to Ruby objects.

2. Generate and migrate databases to define and manage your application's schema.

3. Perform CRUD operations with intuitive Ruby methods.

Active Record is a cornerstone of Rails, and mastering it is essential for creating robust, database-driven applications.

Chapter 7: Building Interactive Views

The views in a Rails application handle the presentation layer, generating HTML that is sent to the user's browser. By building interactive and dynamic views, you can create engaging web pages that adapt to user input and display content in a polished, professional manner. This chapter will guide you through the fundamentals of building interactive views, introduce you to Embedded Ruby (ERB), explain the use of layouts and partials, and show you how to style your application using CSS and Bootstrap.

Introduction to Embedded Ruby (ERB)

Embedded Ruby (ERB) is the default templating system in Rails, allowing you to embed Ruby code within HTML files to dynamically generate content. ERB is easy to use, making it a powerful tool for creating interactive views.

Syntax of ERB

ERB embeds Ruby code within HTML using two types of tags:

1. **Output Tag**: <%= %>
   Outputs the result of Ruby code directly into the HTML.
   Example:

erb

<h1>Welcome, <%= @user.name %>!</h1>

If @user.name is "Alice", the rendered HTML would be:

html

<h1>Welcome, Alice!</h1>

2. **Execution Tag**: <% %>
   Executes Ruby code without outputting anything.
   Example:

erb

<% @users.each do |user| %>

 <p><%= user.name %></p>

<% end %>

This loops through @users and outputs the name of each user.

Using Variables in ERB

In ERB templates, you can access instance variables defined in the corresponding controller. Controller:

ruby

```
class PagesController < ApplicationController
  def home
    @greeting = "Hello, World!"
  end
end
```

View (home.html.erb):

erb

```
<h1><%= @greeting %></h1>
```

Rendered HTML:

html

```
<h1>Hello, World!</h1>
```

Conditional Rendering

ERB supports conditional logic to dynamically modify the content based on certain conditions. Example:

erb

```
<% if @user.admin? %>
  <p>Welcome, Admin!</p>
<% else %>
  <p>Welcome, User!</p>
<% end %>
```

Iterating Through Collections

To render lists of data, you can iterate through collections using loops.
Example:

erb

```
<ul>
```

```erb
<% @posts.each do |post| %>
 <li><%= post.title %></li>
 <% end %>
</ul>
```

Using Layouts and Partials

Rails encourages DRY (Don't Repeat Yourself) principles by promoting reusable code through layouts and partials.

Layouts

A **layout** is a template that wraps around individual views to provide a consistent structure across your application. By default, layouts are stored in app/views/layouts/.

Example: application.html.erb

erb

```
<!DOCTYPE html>
<html>
 <head>
  <title>MyApp</title>
```

```
<%= csrf_meta_tags %>

<%= csp_meta_tag %>

<%= stylesheet_link_tag 'application', media: 'all' %>

<%= javascript_pack_tag 'application' %>
</head>
<body>
 <header>
  <h1>MyApp Header</h1>
 </header>
 <%= yield %>
 <footer>
  <p>&copy; 2025 MyApp</p>
 </footer>
</body>
</html>
```

In this layout, the <%= yield %> tag is a placeholder where the content of individual views will be rendered.

Partials

Partials are reusable snippets of code that can be included in multiple views. They are stored in the app/views/ directory with filenames prefixed by an underscore (_).

Example: _user.html.erb

erb

```
<p><%= user.name %></p>

<p><%= user.email %></p>
```

You can include a partial in a view using the render method:

erb

```
<%= render 'user', user: @user %>
```

Benefits of Layouts and Partials

1. **Consistency**: Layouts ensure that headers, footers, and navigation bars are uniform across all pages.

2. **Reusability**: Partials allow you to avoid duplicating code, making your application easier to maintain.

3. **Clean Code**: Views are more readable and less cluttered.

Styling with CSS and Integrating Bootstrap

While Rails provides the tools to create dynamic views, CSS and front-end frameworks like **Bootstrap** allow you to style your application, making it visually appealing and user-friendly.

Adding Custom CSS to Rails

Rails includes a default directory for stylesheets in app/assets/stylesheets/. You can add custom CSS files to this directory.

Example: app/assets/stylesheets/custom.css

css

```
body {
  font-family: Arial, sans-serif;
}
```

```
h1 {
  color: #3498db;
}
```

Include your CSS file in the application layout:

erb

```erb
<%= stylesheet_link_tag 'custom', media: 'all' %>
```

Using SCSS in Rails

Rails supports SCSS (Sassy CSS), a CSS preprocessor that allows for variables, nesting, and mixins.

Example: app/assets/stylesheets/custom.scss

scss

```scss
$primary-color: #3498db;


body {
  font-family: Arial, sans-serif;
}
```

```
h1 {

  color: $primary-color;

}
```

SCSS makes your stylesheets more maintainable and easier to update.

Integrating Bootstrap

Bootstrap is a popular front-end framework that provides pre-designed components and responsive design utilities. To integrate Bootstrap into your Rails application:

1. **Add Bootstrap via Yarn**:

bash

```
yarn add bootstrap
```

2. **Include Bootstrap in Your Application**: Add the following to app/javascript/packs/application.js:

javascript

```
import "bootstrap";
```

import "../stylesheets/application";

3. **Create a Stylesheet for Bootstrap**: Add the following to app/assets/stylesheets/application.scss:

scss

@import "bootstrap";

Using Bootstrap Components

Bootstrap includes a variety of pre-built components, such as buttons, navigation bars, and modals.
Example: Adding a Bootstrap button

erb

```
<button class="btn btn-primary">Click Me</button>
```

Example: Creating a responsive navigation bar

erb

```
<nav class="navbar navbar-expand-lg navbar-light bg-light">
```

```html
<a class="navbar-brand" href="#">MyApp</a>

<div class="collapse navbar-collapse">

  <ul class="navbar-nav">

    <li class="nav-item"><a class="nav-link" href="/">Home</a></li>

    <li class="nav-item"><a class="nav-link" href="/about">About</a></li>

  </ul>

 </div>

</nav>
```

Customizing Bootstrap

Bootstrap can be customized by overriding its default variables. For example, you can change the primary color:

scss

```scss
$theme-colors: (

  "primary": #ff5733,

);
```

```
@import "bootstrap";
```

Best Practices for Building Interactive Views

1. **Keep Views Simple**: Avoid adding complex logic to views. Use helpers or decorators for advanced functionality.

2. **Use Partials for Reusability**: Break down your views into partials to improve maintainability.

3. **Adopt Responsive Design**: Ensure your application looks great on all devices by using frameworks like Bootstrap.

4. **Optimize Asset Loading**: Use Rails' asset pipeline to manage and compress CSS and JavaScript files for faster loading.

This chapter has provided you with the tools to build engaging and interactive views in Rails. By mastering ERB for dynamic content, leveraging layouts and partials for consistency and reusability, and incorporating CSS and Bootstrap for styling, you can create polished web pages that enhance user experience.

Key takeaways:

- Use Embedded Ruby (ERB) to dynamically generate HTML.

- Employ layouts and partials to keep your views DRY and organized.

- Integrate custom CSS and Bootstrap to create responsive, visually appealing designs.

With these skills, you're ready to build professional-grade views that bring your Rails applications to life.

Chapter 8: Controllers in Depth

In a Ruby on Rails application, controllers are the backbone of your application's logic, managing the interaction between the user, the model, and the view. They process HTTP requests, manage responses, and ensure data security through strong parameters. A well-structured controller is crucial for building scalable and maintainable applications. This chapter dives into the intricacies of Rails controllers, exploring how they handle HTTP requests and responses, the role of strong parameters in security, and best practices for organizing controller actions.

1. Handling HTTP Requests and Responses

At its core, a Rails controller processes incoming HTTP requests and sends back appropriate responses, usually in the form of rendered views or JSON data. Each action in a controller corresponds to a specific HTTP request.

HTTP Methods and RESTful Controllers

Rails controllers are designed to follow the principles of **REST (Representational State Transfer),** mapping HTTP methods to CRUD operations:

HTTP Method	Controller Action	Purpose
GET	index	Retrieve all records
GET	show	Retrieve a single record
GET	new	Display a form for creating a new record
POST	create	Create a new record
GET	edit	Display a form for editing a record
PATCH/PUT	update	Update an existing record
DELETE	destroy	Delete a record

Example: A PostsController for managing blog posts:

ruby

```
class PostsController < ApplicationController
  def index
```

```ruby
    @posts = Post.all
  end


  def show
    @post = Post.find(params[:id])
  end


  def new
    @post = Post.new
  end


  def create
    @post = Post.new(post_params)
    if @post.save
      redirect_to @post
    else
      render :new
    end
  end
```

```ruby
def edit
  @post = Post.find(params[:id])
end


def update
  @post = Post.find(params[:id])
  if @post.update(post_params)
    redirect_to @post
  else
    render :edit
  end
end


def destroy
  @post = Post.find(params[:id])
  @post.destroy
  redirect_to posts_path
end


private
```

```ruby
def post_params

  params.require(:post).permit(:title, :content)

end

end
```

Accessing Request Data

Controllers receive request data via the params hash, which includes:

- **Route Parameters**: Extracted from the URL (e.g., :id in /posts/:id).

- **Query Parameters**: Passed as key-value pairs in the URL (e.g., /posts?category=tech).

- **Form Data**: Submitted via forms.

Example: Accessing parameters:

ruby

```ruby
def show

  @post = Post.find(params[:id]) # Route parameter

end
```

```ruby
def search

 @posts = Post.where(category: params[:category])
# Query parameter

end
```

Managing Responses

Rails controllers send responses back to the client, typically as:

1. **Rendered Views**: HTML pages rendered by default.

ruby

```ruby
def index

 @posts = Post.all

 render :index

end
```

2. **Redirects**: Redirect users to another action or URL.

ruby

```ruby
def create
```

```ruby
if @post.save

  redirect_to @post

else

  render :new

end

end
```

3. **JSON Data**: Useful for APIs.

ruby

```ruby
def show

  @post = Post.find(params[:id])

  render json: @post

end
```

---

2. Strong Parameters and Security

Controllers must ensure that only permitted data is processed by the application. Strong parameters, introduced in Rails 4, help prevent mass assignment vulnerabilities by explicitly specifying which parameters are allowed.

Understanding Mass Assignment Vulnerabilities

Without strong parameters, users could potentially submit data that modifies sensitive attributes, such as admin status.

Example: Insecure parameter handling:

ruby

```ruby
@user = User.new(params[:user])
```

If a malicious user includes admin: true in their form submission, they could gain unauthorized privileges.

Using Strong Parameters

Strong parameters mitigate this risk by requiring developers to whitelist permitted attributes.

Example:

ruby

```ruby
class UsersController < ApplicationController
  def create
    @user = User.new(user_params)
    if @user.save
```

```ruby
    redirect_to @user

  else

    render :new

  end

end


private


def user_params

  params.require(:user).permit(:name, :email,
:password)

  end

end
```

Key points:

1. **require**: Ensures the presence of a specific key (e.g., :user).

2. **permit**: Whitelists attributes that can be assigned.

Nested Parameters

When dealing with nested forms or associations, strong parameters can handle nested attributes.

Example: Permitting nested attributes:

ruby

```ruby
def post_params

 params.require(:post).permit(:title, :content,
comments_attributes: [:id, :content, :_destroy])

end
```

3. Organizing Controller Actions for Scalability

As applications grow, controllers can become bloated and difficult to manage. Following best practices ensures that controllers remain clean, readable, and scalable.

Best Practices for Controller Organization

1. **Adhere to RESTful Conventions**: Stick to standard RESTful actions (index, show, new, etc.) to maintain clarity and consistency.

2. **Use Filters**: Filters like before_action help eliminate repetitive code by running specific methods before or after actions. Example:

ruby

```
class PostsController < ApplicationController
 before_action :set_post, only: [:show, :edit,
:update, :destroy]

 def show; end
 def edit; end

 private

 def set_post
  @post = Post.find(params[:id])
 end
end
```

3. **Extract Logic to Models or Services**: Avoid placing business logic in controllers. Use models or service objects to handle complex operations.

Example: Moving logic to a model:

ruby

```ruby
class Post < ApplicationRecord
  def publish!
    update(published_at: Time.current)
  end
end
```

4. **Paginate Results**: Use gems like kaminari or will_paginate to paginate large datasets.

ruby

```ruby
def index
  @posts = Post.page(params[:page])
end
```

5. **Respond to Different Formats**: Use respond_to to handle multiple response formats (e.g., HTML, JSON, XML).

ruby

```ruby
def show
```

```ruby
@post = Post.find(params[:id])

respond_to do |format|

 format.html

 format.json { render json: @post }

 end

end
```

Refactoring Fat Controllers

Fat controllers are difficult to maintain and test. To refactor:

1. **Use Concerns**: Extract reusable logic into controller concerns. Example:

ruby

```ruby
module SetPost

 extend ActiveSupport::Concern


 included do

 before_action :set_post, only: [:show, :edit]

 end
```

```ruby
def set_post

 @post = Post.find(params[:id])

 end

end
```

2. **Service Objects**: Encapsulate business logic in plain Ruby objects. Example:

ruby

```ruby
class PostPublisher

 def initialize(post)

  @post = post

 end


 def call

  @post.update(published_at: Time.current)

 end

end
```

3. **Presenter or Decorator Pattern**: Use libraries like Draper to manage view-specific logic outside the controller.

4. Advanced Topics in Controllers

Authorization with CanCanCan

Controllers often need to check if users have permission to perform certain actions. Use gems like CanCanCan to handle authorization.

Example:

ruby

```
load_and_authorize_resource
```

Error Handling

Handle errors gracefully to improve user experience:

ruby

```
class ApplicationController <
ActionController::Base

  rescue_from ActiveRecord::RecordNotFound,
with: :record_not_found


  private
```

```ruby
def record_not_found

  render plain: "404 Not Found", status: :not_found

end

end
```

---

5. Testing Controllers

Controller tests ensure that actions behave as expected:

- Use RSpec or Minitest for testing.
- Test responses, redirects, and assigned variables.

Example:

ruby

```ruby
describe PostsController, type: :controller do

  it "renders the index template" do

    get :index

    expect(response).to render_template(:index)

  end

end
```

In this chapter, we've explored the critical role of controllers in Rails applications. You've learned how to:

1. Handle HTTP requests and responses efficiently.

2. Secure your application with strong parameters.

3. Organize controller actions for scalability and maintainability.

With these skills, you can build robust and scalable controllers that serve as the foundation for dynamic, secure, and high-performing Rails applications. In the next chapter, we'll dive deeper into forms and user inputs, further enhancing your ability to create interactive applications.

Chapter 9: Mastering Forms and User Inputs

Forms are one of the most critical components of web applications, serving as the primary mechanism for users to interact with the system. Rails provides robust tools to create forms, validate user input, and handle errors gracefully, ensuring a smooth and secure user experience. This chapter will guide you through building forms using Rails helpers, validating form data to maintain data integrity, and providing intuitive error handling and user feedback.

1. Building Forms with Rails Helpers

Rails simplifies the process of creating forms with its powerful form helpers, which generate HTML form elements while integrating seamlessly with models and controllers. Using these helpers ensures consistency, reduces boilerplate code, and enables easy handling of user input.

1.1 The Basics of Form Helpers

Form helpers are Ruby methods that generate form elements. They are often used in conjunction with models to create dynamic, data-driven forms.

Example: A Simple Form

Here's a basic form for creating a new Post:

erb

```erb
<%= form_with model: @post, local: true do |form| %>
  <p>
   <%= form.label :title %><br>
   <%= form.text_field :title %>
  </p>


  <p>
   <%= form.label :content %><br>
   <%= form.text_area :content %>
  </p>


  <p>
```

```erb
<%= form.submit "Create Post" %>
</p>
<% end %>
```

- **form_with**: Creates a form bound to the @post model.

- **form.label**: Generates a <label> tag for a form field.

- **form.text_field and form.text_area**: Generate input fields for the title and content attributes.

- **form.submit**: Creates a submit button.

1.2 Handling Model Binding

When a form is bound to a model, Rails automatically fills form fields with existing data when editing a record.

Controller:

ruby

```ruby
def edit
  @post = Post.find(params[:id])
end
```

View:

erb

```erb
<%= form_with model: @post, local: true do |form|
%>
  <%= form.text_field :title %>
<% end %>
```

If @post.title is "My Post", the rendered HTML will pre-fill the input field:

html

```html
<input type="text" name="post[title]" id="post_title" value="My Post">
```

1.3 Customizing Form Elements

You can customize form elements by passing options as arguments. For example:

erb

```erb
<%= form.text_field :title, class: "form-control", placeholder: "Enter title" %>
```

This generates:

html

```
<input type="text" name="post[title]" id="post_title"
class="form-control" placeholder="Enter title">
```

1.4 Nested Forms

Rails supports nested attributes, allowing forms to manage associated records.

Model:

ruby

```ruby
class Post < ApplicationRecord
  has_many :comments
  accepts_nested_attributes_for :comments
end
```

Form:

erb

```erb
<%= form_with model: @post, local: true do |form|
%>
```

```
<%= form.fields_for :comments do
|comment_form| %>

  <p>

  <%= comment_form.label :content %><br>

  <%= comment_form.text_area :content %>

  </p>

 <% end %>

<% end %>
```

---

2. Validating Form Data

Validating user input is critical for maintaining data integrity and preventing malicious or invalid data from being saved to the database. Rails provides a rich set of validation helpers that make this process straightforward.

2.1 Adding Validations to Models

Validations are defined in the model to enforce rules on data attributes.

Example: Validating a User model

ruby

```ruby
class User < ApplicationRecord
  validates :name, presence: true
  validates :email, presence: true, uniqueness: true
  validates :password, length: { minimum: 6 }
end
```

2.2 Common Validation Helpers

Rails provides several built-in validation helpers, including:

- **presence**: Ensures the attribute is not blank.
- **uniqueness**: Ensures the attribute is unique across records.
- **length**: Restricts the length of a string.
- **format**: Validates the attribute against a regex pattern.
- **numericality**: Ensures the attribute is a number.

Example: Validating an email format

ruby

```ruby
validates :email, format: { with: URI::MailTo::EMAIL_REGEXP }
```

2.3 Custom Validations

You can define custom validation methods for complex rules.

Example: Validating a username

ruby

```ruby
class User < ApplicationRecord
  validate :valid_username

  private

  def valid_username
    unless name.match?(/\A[a-zA-Z0-9_]+\z/)
      errors.add(:name, "must contain only alphanumeric characters or underscores")
    end
  end
end
```

2.4 Validating Nested Attributes

When using nested forms, validations are also applied to associated models.

Example:

ruby

```ruby
class Post < ApplicationRecord
  has_many :comments
  accepts_nested_attributes_for :comments
  validates_associated :comments
end
```

3. Error Handling and User Feedback

Effective error handling and user feedback improve the user experience by guiding users to correct their mistakes.

3.1 Displaying Error Messages

Rails provides the errors object to list validation errors for a model.

Example: Displaying errors in a form

erb

```erb
<% if @post.errors.any? %>
  <div class="error-messages">
    <h2><%= pluralize(@post.errors.count, "error") %> prevented this post from being saved:</h2>
    <ul>
      <% @post.errors.full_messages.each do |message| %>
        <li><%= message %></li>
      <% end %>
    </ul>
  </div>
<% end %>
```

This might render:

html

```html
<div class="error-messages">
  <h2>2 errors prevented this post from being saved:</h2>
  <ul>
```

```
<li>Title can't be blank</li>
```

```
<li>Content can't be blank</li>
```

```
 </ul>
```

```
</div>
```

3.2 Highlighting Invalid Fields

You can highlight invalid form fields to visually indicate errors.

Example: Adding error class to invalid fields

erb

```erb
<p>
  <%= form.label :title %><br>
  <%= form.text_field :title, class: @post.errors[:title].any? ? "error" : "" %>
</p>
```

CSS:

css

```css
.error {
  border-color: red;
```

```
}
```

3.3 Flash Messages

Flash messages provide user feedback for actions like successful form submissions or errors.

Controller:

ruby

```ruby
def create
  @post = Post.new(post_params)
  if @post.save
    flash[:notice] = "Post was successfully created."
    redirect_to @post
  else
    flash[:alert] = "There was an error creating the post."
    render :new
  end
end
```

View (application.html.erb):

erb

```
<% if flash[:notice] %>

  <div class="flash notice"><%= flash[:notice]
%></div>

<% elsif flash[:alert] %>

  <div class="flash alert"><%= flash[:alert] %></div>

<% end %>
```

3.4 Client-Side Validation

While Rails focuses on server-side validation, you can enhance forms with client-side validation using JavaScript libraries like ClientSideValidations or frameworks like Stimulus.

Example: Adding client-side validation

javascript

```
document.addEventListener("DOMContentLoaded
", function () {

  const form = document.querySelector("form");

  form.addEventListener("submit", function (event) {

    const titleField =
document.querySelector("#post_title");
```

```
if (titleField.value.trim() === "") {

  alert("Title can't be blank");

  event.preventDefault();

}

});

});
```

4. Best Practices for Forms and User Inputs

1. **Keep Forms Simple**: Only include necessary fields to avoid overwhelming users.

2. **Use Strong Parameters**: Always whitelist input attributes to prevent mass assignment vulnerabilities.

3. **Provide Real-Time Feedback**: Use JavaScript to validate inputs dynamically.

4. **Be Accessible**: Ensure forms are usable for people with disabilities by using proper labels and ARIA attributes.

5. **Sanitize Inputs**: Clean user input to prevent SQL injection and XSS attacks.

In this chapter, you've learned how to create robust and user-friendly forms in Rails. By leveraging Rails helpers, validating user input, and implementing effective error handling, you can build forms that are secure, intuitive, and interactive. These skills are crucial for creating dynamic web applications that prioritize user experience and data integrity.

Chapter 10: Authentication and Authorization

Authentication and authorization are essential for securing web applications. Authentication verifies the identity of a user, while authorization determines what actions and resources a user has permission to access. This chapter focuses on implementing authentication using the popular Devise gem, setting up role-based access control (RBAC), and protecting sensitive routes and actions in a Ruby on Rails application.

---

1. Implementing User Authentication with Devise

Devise is a robust and flexible authentication solution for Rails applications. It provides a wealth of features, including user registration, login, password recovery, and more.

1.1 Installing Devise

1. Add Devise to your Gemfile:

ruby

gem 'devise'

2. Install the gem:

bash

bundle install

3. Run the Devise installer:

bash

rails generate devise:install

The installer configures Devise for your application and creates an initializer file at config/initializers/devise.rb. It also provides instructions for adding flash messages and setting up mailer defaults.

1.2 Generating a User Model

To create a User model with Devise, run:

bash

rails generate devise User

This generates:

- A User model in app/models/user.rb with Devise modules.

- A migration file to add necessary columns to the users table.

Run the migration:

bash

rails db:migrate

1.3 Configuring Devise Modules

Devise includes various modules to customize authentication behavior. Common modules include:

- **Database Authenticatable**: Handles user login and password encryption.

- **Registerable**: Allows user registration.

- **Recoverable**: Enables password recovery.

- **Confirmable**: Requires email confirmation for account activation.

- **Trackable**: Tracks user sign-in statistics (e.g., IP address, sign-in count).

Enable or disable modules in the User model:

ruby

```ruby
class User < ApplicationRecord
  devise :database_authenticatable, :registerable,
       :recoverable, :rememberable, :validatable
end
```

1.4 Adding Authentication to Views

Generate Devise views to customize user-facing forms and pages:

bash

```bash
rails generate devise:views
```

This creates view templates in app/views/devise/, including:

- registrations/new.html.erb for sign-up.
- sessions/new.html.erb for login.

1.5 Securing Routes and Controllers

Devise provides helper methods to manage authentication:

- **authenticate_user!**: Ensures a user is logged in before accessing a controller action. Example:

ruby

class PostsController < ApplicationController

 before_action :authenticate_user!, only: [:new, :create]

end

- **current_user**: Returns the currently logged-in user.

- **user_signed_in?**: Checks if a user is logged in.

1.6 Customizing Devise

You can customize Devise to fit your application's needs:

- **Mailer Configuration**: Set up email for password recovery and confirmation in config/environments/development.rb:

ruby

```
config.action_mailer.default_url_options = { host: 'localhost', port: 3000 }
```

- **Routes Customization**: Modify Devise routes in config/routes.rb:

ruby

```
devise_for :users, path: 'auth', path_names: { sign_in: 'login', sign_out: 'logout' }
```

---

2. Setting Up Role-Based Access Control (RBAC)

Role-based access control (RBAC) is a method of restricting access based on user roles. In a Rails application, roles such as admin, moderator, and regular user can dictate what resources and actions each user can access.

2.1 Adding Roles to the User Model

Add a role column to the users table:

bash

```
rails generate migration AddRoleToUsers role:string
rails db:migrate
```

Define roles in the User model:

ruby

```
class User < ApplicationRecord
  devise :database_authenticatable, :registerable,
     :recoverable, :rememberable, :validatable

  ROLES = %w[admin moderator user].freeze

  def admin?
   role == 'admin'
  end

  def moderator?
```

```ruby
    role == 'moderator'
  end


  def user?
    role == 'user'
  end
end
```

2.2 Assigning Roles

Roles can be assigned during user creation or updated later via admin panels.

Example: Assign a role during sign-up:

ruby

```ruby
def create
  @user = User.new(user_params)
  @user.role = 'user' # Default role
  if @user.save
    redirect_to @user
  else
```

```
  render :new

 end

end
```

2.3 Restricting Access Based on Roles

Use helper methods to check roles and restrict actions:

ruby

```ruby
class AdminController < ApplicationController

  before_action :authenticate_user!

  before_action :authorize_admin


  private


  def authorize_admin

    redirect_to root_path, alert: 'Access denied' unless current_user.admin?

  end

end
```

2.4 Using Authorization Gems

Authorization gems like **Pundit** and **CanCanCan** simplify managing permissions.

- **Pundit**: Install Pundit:

bash

```
bundle add pundit
```

Generate a policy:

bash

```
rails generate pundit:policy Post
```

Define access rules in the policy:

ruby

```
class PostPolicy
  attr_reader :user, :post

  def initialize(user, post)
    @user = user
    @post = post
```

```
  end


  def edit?

    user.admin? || post.user == user

  end

end
```

Apply policies in controllers:

ruby

```
def edit

  @post = Post.find(params[:id])

  authorize @post

end
```

---

3. Protecting Sensitive Routes and Actions

Sensitive routes and actions, such as admin dashboards and user management, must be secured to prevent unauthorized access.

3.1 Using before_action Filters

Use before_action in controllers to protect specific actions:

ruby

```ruby
class AdminController < ApplicationController
  before_action :authenticate_user!
  before_action :authorize_admin

  private

  def authorize_admin
    redirect_to root_path, alert: 'Access denied' unless current_user.admin?
  end
end
```

3.2 Protecting Routes

Use route constraints to restrict access to specific user roles:

ruby

```ruby
constraints ->(req) {
req.env['warden'].user&.admin? } do

  namespace :admin do

    resources :dashboard

  end

end
```

3.3 Preventing Unauthorized Actions

Ensure actions are protected by adding checks in controllers:

ruby

```ruby
def destroy

  if current_user.admin?

    @post.destroy

    redirect_to posts_path, notice: 'Post deleted'

  else

    redirect_to posts_path, alert: 'Not authorized'

  end

end
```

3.4 Securing APIs

If your application provides APIs, ensure endpoints are secured with authentication tokens or session-based authentication. Devise provides a **Token Authenticatable** module for token-based access.

Example: Token authentication for an API:

ruby

```ruby
class Api::V1::PostsController < Api::BaseController
  before_action :authenticate_user!

  def index
    render json: Post.all
  end
end
```

4. Best Practices for Authentication and Authorization

1. **Use HTTPS**: Always serve your application over HTTPS to secure data transmission.

2. **Limit Sensitive Data Exposure**: Avoid exposing sensitive user data like passwords in views or logs.

3. **Follow the Principle of Least Privilege**: Grant users only the permissions they need.

4. **Audit Logs**: Maintain logs of user actions for accountability and debugging.

5. **Regularly Test Authorization Rules**: Ensure that users cannot bypass role restrictions or access unauthorized resources.

Authentication and authorization are cornerstones of secure web applications. In this chapter, you've learned:

1. How to implement user authentication using Devise.

2. How to set up role-based access control (RBAC) to manage permissions.

3. Techniques for protecting sensitive routes and actions.

By integrating these features into your Rails application, you can provide a secure and user-friendly environment while safeguarding sensitive data and actions. As you continue building, these foundational skills will enable you to handle increasingly complex access control scenarios.

Chapter 11: Advanced Database Features

Databases form the backbone of most web applications, providing a robust system for storing, retrieving, and managing data. Rails, through Active Record, offers a range of powerful tools to manage database relationships, perform complex queries, and optimize database performance. This chapter dives deep into these advanced features, focusing on associations, joins, scopes, and performance optimization techniques that allow your application to scale effectively while maintaining speed and reliability.

1. Associations and Relationships in Active Record

Associations define the relationships between models in Rails. By leveraging Active Record's association methods, you can simplify database interactions and represent relationships in an intuitive, object-oriented way.

1.1 Types of Associations

Active Record supports several types of associations:

1. **One-to-One**
   Example: A User has one Profile.

ruby

```
class User < ApplicationRecord
  has_one :profile
end


class Profile < ApplicationRecord
  belongs_to :user
end
```

Usage:

ruby

```
user = User.find(1)

profile = user.profile
```

2. **One-to-Many**
   Example: A Post has many Comments.

ruby

```ruby
class Post < ApplicationRecord
  has_many :comments
end

class Comment < ApplicationRecord
  belongs_to :post
end
```

Usage:

ruby

```ruby
post = Post.find(1)
comments = post.comments
```

3. **Many-to-Many**
   Example: A Post has many Tags, and a Tag has many Posts.

ruby

```ruby
class Post < ApplicationRecord
  has_and_belongs_to_many :tags
```

```ruby
end
```

```ruby
class Tag < ApplicationRecord
  has_and_belongs_to_many :posts
end
```

Usage:

ruby

```ruby
post = Post.find(1)
tags = post.tags
```

4. **Self-Referential**
   Example: A Category can have many subcategories and belong to one parent category.

ruby

```ruby
class Category < ApplicationRecord
  has_many :subcategories, class_name: 'Category', foreign_key: 'parent_id'
  belongs_to :parent_category, class_name: 'Category', optional: true
end
```

1.2 Options for Associations

Active Record associations support options that modify their behavior:

- **dependent**: Determines what happens to associated records when a parent is deleted.

ruby

```
has_many :comments, dependent: :destroy
```

- **through**: Specifies a join model for many-to-many relationships.

ruby

```
class Physician < ApplicationRecord
  has_many :appointments
  has_many :patients, through: :appointments
end
```

- **inverse_of**: Maintains consistency in bidirectional associations.

ruby

```ruby
class Post < ApplicationRecord
  has_many :comments, inverse_of: :post
end
```

2. Using Joins and Scopes for Complex Queries

While associations simplify database interactions, complex queries often require using **joins** and **scopes** to fetch related data efficiently.

2.1 Joins in Active Record

Joins are used to combine data from multiple tables. Active Record provides several methods for creating joins:

1. **joins**: Performs an inner join.

ruby

```ruby
Post.joins(:comments).where(comments: { approved: true })
```

2. **includes**: Preloads associations to avoid N+1 query problems.

ruby

```ruby
Post.includes(:comments).each do |post|

  post.comments.each { |comment| puts
comment.content }

end
```

3. **eager_load**: Combines preloading and joining, often for conditions on associated records.

ruby

```ruby
Post.eager_load(:comments).where(comments: {
approved: true })
```

4. **left_outer_joins**: Fetches records even when associated records don't exist.

ruby

```ruby
Post.left_outer_joins(:comments).where(comment
s: { id: nil })
```

2.2 Scopes for Reusable Queries

Scopes encapsulate commonly used queries, making them reusable and readable.

Example: Defining a scope

ruby

```ruby
class Post < ApplicationRecord
  scope :published, -> { where(published: true) }
  scope :recent, -> { order(created_at: :desc).limit(5) }
end
```

Usage:

ruby

```ruby
Post.published.recent
```

Scopes can also accept arguments:

ruby

```ruby
scope :created_before, ->(date) { where('created_at < ?', date) }
```

2.3 Combining Joins and Scopes

Joins and scopes can be combined for advanced queries. For example:

ruby

```
Post.joins(:comments).merge(Comment.approved)
```

---

3. Optimizing Database Performance

As applications grow, database queries can become a bottleneck. Rails provides several strategies and tools to optimize performance, ensuring scalability and efficiency.

3.1 Avoiding N+1 Queries

The N+1 query problem occurs when a query is executed for each associated record, leading to inefficiency. Use includes to solve this issue.

Example: Problematic query

ruby

```
Post.all.each do |post|
  puts post.comments.count
end
```

Solution:

ruby

```ruby
Post.includes(:comments).each do |post|

 puts post.comments.count

end
```

3.2 Indexing

Database indexes speed up queries by reducing the search space for lookups. Add indexes to frequently queried columns.

Example: Adding an index

bash

```bash
rails generate migration AddIndexToPostsTitle
```

Migration file:

ruby

```ruby
class AddIndexToPostsTitle <
ActiveRecord::Migration[6.1]

 def change

  add_index :posts, :title

 end
```

end

Run the migration:

bash

rails db:migrate

3.3 Caching

Caching stores the results of expensive queries to reduce database load. Rails supports several caching mechanisms:

1. **Query Caching**: Enabled by default in Rails.

2. **Fragment Caching**: Caches parts of a view.

erb

```erb
<% cache @post do %>
  <%= render @post %>
<% end %>
```

3. **Low-Level Caching**: Stores arbitrary data.

ruby

```ruby
Rails.cache.write('key', 'value')
```

```
Rails.cache.read('key')
```

3.4 Database Connection Pooling

Connection pooling reuses database connections, improving efficiency in multi-threaded environments. Configure pooling in config/database.yml:

yaml

production:

  pool: 10

3.5 Using Background Jobs

For time-consuming database operations, use background jobs to offload work to a queue.

Example: Using Active Job with Sidekiq

ruby

```ruby
class ArchiveOldPostsJob < ApplicationJob
  queue_as :default
```

```ruby
def perform

  Post.where('created_at < ?',
1.year.ago).update_all(archived: true)

  end

end
```

3.6 Query Optimization

1. **Select Specific Columns**: Avoid fetching unnecessary data.

ruby

```ruby
Post.select(:title, :created_at)
```

2. **Batch Processing**: Use find_each for large datasets.

ruby

```ruby
Post.find_each(batch_size: 100) do |post|

  process(post)

end
```

3. **Use Raw SQL for Complex Queries**: For highly optimized queries, write raw SQL.

ruby

```
Post.find_by_sql('SELECT * FROM posts WHERE
published = true')
```

4. Best Practices for Advanced Database Features

1. **Normalize Relationships**: Use appropriate associations to reflect real-world relationships.

2. **Encapsulate Queries in Scopes**: Keep controllers and views clean by moving logic to models.

3. **Monitor Database Performance**: Use tools like pgHero or New Relic to analyze query performance.

4. **Test for Edge Cases**: Ensure your application handles edge cases, such as missing or invalid data.

In this chapter, you've explored advanced database features in Rails. By mastering associations, joins, scopes, and performance optimization techniques, you can build robust, scalable, and efficient applications. Key takeaways include:

- Leveraging associations to define intuitive model relationships.

- Using joins and scopes to perform complex and reusable queries.

- Optimizing database performance through indexing, caching, and efficient querying.

These skills are crucial as your application grows in complexity and user base, ensuring a seamless experience for users while maintaining optimal performance.

Chapter 12: Working with APIs

APIs (Application Programming Interfaces) play a crucial role in modern web development, enabling applications to communicate and exchange data. In Rails, you can seamlessly consume external APIs to integrate third-party data and build your own APIs to expose your application's functionality. Additionally, Rails supports GraphQL, a powerful query language for APIs, offering flexibility in data fetching. This chapter provides an in-depth guide to consuming external APIs, building APIs with Rails, and introduces GraphQL for crafting advanced APIs.

1. Consuming External APIs with Rails

Consuming external APIs allows you to integrate third-party services such as payment gateways, weather data, or social media platforms into your application.

1.1 Making HTTP Requests

The first step in consuming APIs is making HTTP requests. The most popular Ruby gem for this is

HTTParty, though Rails' built-in Net::HTTP or Faraday can also be used.

Installing HTTParty: Add the gem to your Gemfile:

ruby

```
gem 'httparty'
```

Install the gem:

bash

```
bundle install
```

1.2 Fetching Data from an API

Example: Consuming a weather API

ruby

```
require 'httparty'

class WeatherService
  include HTTParty
  base_uri 'api.openweathermap.org'
```

```ruby
  def initialize(api_key)

    @options = { query: { appid: api_key, units:
'metric' } }

  end


  def fetch_weather(city)

    self.class.get("/data/2.5/weather?q=#{city}",
@options)

  end
end
```

```ruby
# Usage

service = WeatherService.new('<YOUR_API_KEY>')

response = service.fetch_weather('London')

puts response.parsed_response
```

Key methods:

- **get**: Makes an HTTP GET request.

- **post**: Makes an HTTP POST request.

- **parsed_response**: Parses the JSON
  response into a Ruby hash.

1.3 Handling API Responses

API responses may include errors or unexpected data. Handle these gracefully to ensure a robust application.

Example: Error handling in an API call:

ruby

```ruby
response = service.fetch_weather('InvalidCity')

if response.success?

  puts response.parsed_response

else

  puts "Error: #{response.code} - #{response.message}"

end
```

1.4 Storing API Data

For frequently accessed data, consider storing the API response in your database or using caching to reduce redundant API calls.

Example: Caching API responses with Rails:

ruby

```
Rails.cache.fetch("weather_#{city}", expires_in:
1.hour) do

  service.fetch_weather(city).parsed_response

end
```

2. Building Your Own APIs Using Rails

Rails makes it easy to build RESTful APIs by using its MVC framework to expose application data as JSON or XML.

2.1 Setting Up a Rails API

Rails provides an API-only mode for building lightweight APIs:

bash

```
rails new MyAPI --api
```

This creates a minimal Rails application optimized for API development, excluding unnecessary components like view templates.

2.2 Creating API Endpoints

To expose data through an API, use Rails controllers to handle requests and render JSON responses.

Example: Creating an API for posts

ruby

```ruby
class Api::V1::PostsController < ApplicationController
  def index
    @posts = Post.all
    render json: @posts
  end

  def show
    @post = Post.find(params[:id])
    render json: @post
  end
end
```

Routes:

ruby

```
namespace :api do

 namespace :v1 do

  resources :posts, only: [:index, :show]

 end

end
```

2.3 Serializing Data

Use the **ActiveModel Serializers** gem to control how data is formatted in your API.

Installing ActiveModel Serializers:

bash

```
gem 'active_model_serializers'

bundle install
```

Defining a Serializer:

ruby

```
class PostSerializer < ActiveModel::Serializer

 attributes :id, :title, :content, :created_at

end
```

Using the Serializer:

ruby

```
render json: @post, serializer: PostSerializer
```

2.4 Handling Authentication

APIs often require authentication. Common methods include:

1. **API Keys**: Clients include an API key in their requests.

ruby

```
class ApplicationController < ActionController::API

  before_action :authenticate


  private


  def authenticate
    render json: { error: 'Unauthorized' }, status: :unauthorized unless valid_api_key?
  end
```

```ruby
def valid_api_key?

  request.headers['Authorization'] ==
ENV['API_KEY']

  end

end
```

2. **Token-Based Authentication**: Use libraries like devise-jwt for secure token authentication.

2.5 Versioning Your API

Versioning ensures backward compatibility as your API evolves. Use namespaces for versioning:

ruby

```ruby
namespace :api do

  namespace :v1 do

    resources :posts

  end

end
```

2.6 Pagination

For APIs that return large datasets, use gems like kaminari to paginate results.

Example:

ruby

```ruby
def index

  @posts = Post.page(params[:page]).per(10)

  render json: @posts

end
```

3. Introduction to GraphQL with Rails

GraphQL is a query language for APIs that allows clients to request specific data. Unlike REST, GraphQL provides a single endpoint for all queries and supports nested and related data fetching.

3.1 Setting Up GraphQL in Rails

Install the graphql gem:

bash

```
gem 'graphql'
```

```
bundle install
```

```
rails generate graphql:install
```

This creates:

- A GraphQL schema in app/graphql/.

- A GraphqlController to handle requests.

3.2 Defining a Schema

A GraphQL schema defines the structure of the data your API provides.

Example: Defining a PostType

ruby

```ruby
class Types::PostType < Types::BaseObject
  field :id, ID, null: false
  field :title, String, null: false
  field :content, String, null: true
  field :created_at, String, null: false
end
```

Add the type to the schema:

ruby

```ruby
class Types::QueryType < Types::BaseObject
  field :posts, [Types::PostType], null: false

  def posts
    Post.all
  end
end
```

3.3 Querying Data

Clients query data using the GraphQL query language.

Example: Querying posts

graphql

```graphql
query {
  posts {
    id
    title
```

```
    content

  }

}
```

Response:

json

```
{

  "data": {

    "posts": [

      { "id": "1", "title": "First Post", "content": "Hello,
world!" }

    ]

  }

}
```

3.4 Adding Mutations

Mutations allow clients to modify data.

Example: Adding a mutation for creating posts

ruby

```ruby
class Mutations::CreatePost <
Mutations::BaseMutation

  argument :title, String, required: true

  argument :content, String, required: true


  field :post, Types::PostType, null: false


  def resolve(title:, content:)
    post = Post.create!(title: title, content: content)
    { post: post }
  end
end
```

Add the mutation to the schema:

ruby

```ruby
class Types::MutationType < Types::BaseObject

  field :create_post, mutation:
Mutations::CreatePost

end
```

Client mutation:

graphql

```
mutation {

  createPost(title: "New Post", content: "GraphQL is
awesome!") {

    post {

      id

      title

    }

  }

}
```

3.5 Benefits of GraphQL

1. **Flexible Queries**: Clients request only the data they need.

2. **Single Endpoint**: Reduces the need for multiple endpoints.

3. **Nested Data**: Fetch related data in a single query.

4. **Versionless**: GraphQL APIs evolve without breaking existing clients.

4. Best Practices for APIs

1. **Secure Your API**: Use HTTPS and validate all inputs.

2. **Handle Errors Gracefully**: Return meaningful error messages with appropriate status codes.

3. **Rate Limiting**: Prevent abuse by limiting the number of API requests.

4. **Documentation**: Use tools like Swagger or GraphiQL for clear API documentation.

5. **Monitor Performance**: Use tools like Skylight or New Relic to monitor API performance.

In this chapter, you've explored:

1. **Consuming External APIs**: Integrating third-party data into your application.

2. **Building Your Own APIs**: Creating RESTful APIs with Rails and enhancing them with features like authentication and serialization.

3. **Introducing GraphQL**: Building flexible, efficient APIs using GraphQL.

By mastering these techniques, you'll be equipped to build robust, scalable, and secure APIs that integrate seamlessly with modern applications. Whether consuming or providing APIs, these skills are invaluable in the interconnected world of web development.

Chapter 13: Testing and Debugging

Testing and debugging are critical to building robust and reliable web applications. In Rails, a variety of tools and techniques are available to ensure that your code functions as intended and to identify and resolve issues efficiently. This chapter provides a comprehensive guide to writing unit, integration, and system tests, debugging common Rails issues, and using tools like RSpec and Capybara to streamline the development process.

1. Writing Unit, Integration, and System Tests

Testing in Rails ensures that your application behaves as expected. Rails provides a built-in testing framework based on **Minitest**, while libraries like **RSpec** and **Capybara** extend its capabilities.

1.1 Unit Testing

Unit tests focus on individual models, methods, or components, ensuring that each piece of code works correctly in isolation.

Example: Testing a Model

For a Post model with validations:

ruby

```ruby
class Post < ApplicationRecord
  validates :title, presence: true
end
```

Test file: test/models/post_test.rb

ruby

```ruby
require "test_helper"

class PostTest < ActiveSupport::TestCase
  test "should not save post without title" do
    post = Post.new
    assert_not post.save, "Saved the post without a title"
  end

  test "should save valid post" do
```

```ruby
post = Post.new(title: "Test Post")

assert post.save, "Failed to save a valid post"

end

end
```

1.2 Integration Testing

Integration tests check how different parts of your application work together, such as models, controllers, and views.

Example: Testing a Workflow

For a PostsController with an index action:

ruby

```ruby
class PostsController < ApplicationController

  def index

    @posts = Post.all

  end

end
```

Test file: test/controllers/posts_controller_test.rb

ruby

```ruby
require "test_helper"


class PostsControllerTest <
ActionDispatch::IntegrationTest
  test "should get index" do
    get posts_url
    assert_response :success
    assert_select "h1", "Posts"
  end
end
```

1.3 System Testing

System tests simulate user interactions in a browser, testing the entire application workflow. Rails integrates **Capybara** for writing system tests.

Example: Testing a User Journey

Test file: test/system/posts_test.rb

ruby

```ruby
require "application_system_test_case"
```

```ruby
class PostsTest < ApplicationSystemTestCase
  test "visiting the index" do
    visit posts_url
    assert_selector "h1", text: "Posts"
  end

  test "creating a post" do
    visit posts_url
    click_on "New Post"
    fill_in "Title", with: "New Post Title"
    click_on "Create Post"
    assert_text "Post was successfully created"
  end
end
```

2. Debugging Common Rails Issues

Debugging is an essential part of development, allowing you to identify and resolve issues in your application. Rails provides several tools and techniques to make debugging easier.

2.1 Debugging Techniques

1. **Rails Logs**
   Rails logs provide detailed information about requests, database queries, and errors. Logs are located in log/development.log for the development environment.

Example: Searching logs for specific errors

bash

```
tail -f log/development.log
```

2. **Debugging with byebug**
   The byebug gem allows you to pause code execution and inspect variables.

Example:

ruby

```
class PostsController < ApplicationController
  def index
    byebug
    @posts = Post.all
  end
```

end

When the code reaches the byebug line, it pauses execution, and you can inspect variables or step through the code.

3. **Using the Rails Console**
   The Rails console (rails console) lets you interact with your application in a live environment. You can query the database, test methods, or debug issues.

Example:

ruby

Post.find(1)

4. **Stack Traces**
   Rails displays stack traces for errors in the development environment, showing the exact location of issues. Review the stack trace to identify problematic code.

2.2 Common Issues and Solutions

1. **N+1 Query Problem**
   Symptom: Multiple database queries are executed for associated records.

Solution: Use includes to eager load associations.

ruby

```ruby
Post.includes(:comments).each do |post|

 puts post.comments.size

end
```

2. **Unpermitted Parameters**
   Symptom: Strong parameters reject submitted data.
   Solution: Permit the required parameters in the controller.

ruby

```ruby
params.require(:post).permit(:title, :content)
```

3. **Missing Migrations**
   Symptom: Application errors due to missing database schema changes.
   Solution: Run pending migrations.

bash

```bash
rails db:migrate
```

4. **Routing Errors**
   Symptom: "No route matches" error.
   Solution: Verify routes in config/routes.rb
   and run rails routes to inspect defined
   routes.

---

3. Using Tools like RSpec and Capybara

While Rails includes Minitest by default, many
developers prefer **RSpec** for its expressive syntax
and **Capybara** for integration testing.

3.1 RSpec

RSpec is a popular testing framework for Ruby and
Rails applications.

Installing RSpec

Add the following gems to your Gemfile:

ruby

group :development, :test do

 gem 'rspec-rails'

end

Run the installation:

bash

bundle install

rails generate rspec:install

Writing RSpec Tests

Model Test:

ruby

```ruby
require 'rails_helper'

RSpec.describe Post, type: :model do
  it "is valid with a title" do
    post = Post.new(title: "RSpec Test")
    expect(post).to be_valid
  end

  it "is invalid without a title" do
    post = Post.new(title: nil)
    expect(post).to_not be_valid
```

end

end

Controller Test:

ruby

require 'rails_helper'

RSpec.describe PostsController, type: :controller do
  describe "GET index" do
    it "returns a success response" do
      get :index
      expect(response).to be_successful
    end
  end
end

3.2 Capybara

Capybara simulates user interactions with your application in system tests.

Installing Capybara

Add the gem to your Gemfile:

ruby

```
gem 'capybara'
```

Set up Capybara in your test environment:

ruby

```
require 'capybara/rails'
```

Writing Capybara Tests

ruby

```
require 'rails_helper'

RSpec.feature "Posts", type: :feature do
  scenario "User creates a new post" do
    visit "/posts"
    click_link "New Post"
    fill_in "Title", with: "Capybara Test"
    click_button "Create Post"
```

```ruby
  expect(page).to have_text("Post was successfully
created")
 end

end
```

3.3 Combining RSpec and Capybara

RSpec and Capybara work seamlessly together to provide a comprehensive testing framework.

Example: Feature test with RSpec and Capybara

ruby

```ruby
RSpec.feature "Posts", type: :feature do
 scenario "User views a post" do
   post = Post.create(title: "Test Post", content: "Test
Content")
   visit "/posts/#{post.id}"
   expect(page).to have_text("Test Post")
   expect(page).to have_text("Test Content")
  end
end
```

4. Best Practices for Testing and Debugging

1. **Write Tests First**: Use Test-Driven Development (TDD) to guide your coding process.

2. **Keep Tests Isolated**: Ensure tests do not rely on external systems or shared data.

3. **Test Edge Cases**: Write tests for edge cases and potential user errors.

4. **Use Factories**: Use libraries like **FactoryBot** to generate test data.

ruby

```ruby
FactoryBot.define do
  factory :post do
    title { "Test Post" }
    content { "Test Content" }
  end
end
```

5. **Regularly Run Tests**: Run tests frequently to catch issues early.

6. **Debug with Logs and Breakpoints**: Use logs and byebug strategically to pinpoint issues.

This chapter covered the essentials of testing and debugging in Rails. Key takeaways include:

- Writing unit, integration, and system tests to ensure application reliability.

- Debugging techniques to identify and resolve issues effectively.

- Leveraging tools like RSpec and Capybara to enhance your testing workflow.

By following these practices, you'll create robust, maintainable applications and streamline your development process. Testing and debugging are not just development chores—they are fundamental to delivering high-quality software.

Chapter 14: Background Jobs and Task Automation

Modern web applications often require tasks to be executed in the background or at scheduled intervals. These could include sending emails, processing uploads, or generating reports—tasks that are better handled asynchronously to improve user experience and system performance. Rails provides robust solutions like **Active Job** for a unified interface and **Sidekiq** for high-performance background processing. Coupled with tools like **Cron** and **Whenever**, Rails makes it easy to schedule and manage recurring tasks. This chapter explores these tools in depth, focusing on how to set up, use, and optimize them for your application.

1. Introduction to Active Job and Sidekiq

Rails' built-in **Active Job** framework and the third-party library **Sidekiq** allow developers to manage background jobs seamlessly.

1.1 What Are Background Jobs?

Background jobs enable certain tasks to run asynchronously or outside the main request-response cycle. For example:

- Sending welcome emails after user registration.
- Processing file uploads.
- Sending notifications to users.

By offloading these tasks to the background, you:

1. Improve user experience by reducing wait times.
2. Enhance application scalability by distributing workloads.

1.2 Active Job Overview

Active Job is a Rails framework for managing background jobs, providing a consistent interface to various job-processing libraries (e.g., Sidekiq, Resque, Delayed Job).

Creating a Job

Generate a new job with:

bash

rails generate job MyJob

This creates a file in app/jobs/:

ruby

```ruby
class MyJob < ApplicationJob
  queue_as :default

  def perform(*args)
    # Perform the task here
    puts "Performing background job with args: #{args.inspect}"
  end
end
```

Enqueuing a Job

You can enqueue a job to run in the background:

ruby

```ruby
MyJob.perform_later("Hello", "World")
```

1.3 Setting Up Sidekiq

While Active Job provides a consistent interface, **Sidekiq** is one of the most popular libraries for job processing due to its speed and scalability. Sidekiq uses **Redis** to manage background job queues.

Installing Sidekiq

1. Add Sidekiq to your Gemfile:

ruby

```
gem 'sidekiq'
```

2. Install Redis:

bash

```
brew install redis   # macOS
sudo apt-get install redis-server  # Ubuntu
```

3. Start the Redis server:

bash

```
redis-server
```

4. Configure Rails to use Sidekiq with Active Job:

ruby

```
# config/application.rb
config.active_job.queue_adapter = :sidekiq
```

5. Define a Sidekiq worker:

ruby

```
class MyWorker
  include Sidekiq::Worker

  def perform(*args)
    puts "Processing with Sidekiq: #{args.inspect}"
  end
end
```

6. Enqueue a job:

ruby

```
MyWorker.perform_async("Hello", "World")
```

1.4 Monitoring Jobs with Sidekiq Web

Sidekiq provides a web interface to monitor job queues, retries, and failures.

Enable the web interface:

ruby

```
# config/routes.rb

require 'sidekiq/web'

mount Sidekiq::Web => '/sidekiq'
```

Access it at http://localhost:3000/sidekiq.

---

2. Scheduling Tasks with Cron and Whenever

Some tasks need to run on a fixed schedule (e.g., nightly database backups, weekly email reports). **Cron** is a Unix-based tool for scheduling tasks, and the **Whenever** gem integrates Cron with Rails.

2.1 Understanding Cron

Cron jobs are defined in the **crontab** file. Each line specifies a schedule and the command to execute:

bash

```
# Run at 2:30 AM every day

30 2 * * * /path/to/command
```

2.2 Setting Up Whenever

The **Whenever** gem provides a Ruby-friendly DSL to define Cron jobs for your Rails application.

Installing Whenever

Add the gem to your Gemfile:

ruby

gem 'whenever', require: false

Install the gem:

bash

bundle install

Generate the schedule file:

bash

wheneverize .

This creates a config/schedule.rb file.

2.3 Defining Scheduled Tasks

Use the schedule.rb file to define tasks.

Example: Send daily reports

ruby

```
every 1.day, at: '2:30 am' do
  runner "ReportMailer.send_daily_report"
end
```

Example: Run a rake task every hour

ruby

```
every :hour do
  rake "cleanup:tmp_files"
end
```

Update the Cron job:

bash

```
whenever --update-crontab
```

2.4 Viewing and Removing Cron Jobs

View the current crontab:

bash

```
crontab -l
```

Remove all Cron jobs:

bash

```
crontab -r
```

3. Managing Long-Running Tasks Efficiently

Some tasks, such as processing large datasets or running machine learning models, can take considerable time. Efficiently managing these tasks ensures that they don't block other operations.

3.1 Batch Processing

Divide long-running tasks into smaller batches to avoid overloading the system.

Example: Process records in batches

ruby

```
User.find_in_batches(batch_size: 100) do |batch|
  batch.each do |user|
    MyJob.perform_later(user.id)
  end
end
```

3.2 Retry Strategies

Background jobs can fail due to temporary issues (e.g., network errors). Implement retry strategies to handle such cases.

Sidekiq retries failed jobs automatically. Customize the retry behavior:

ruby

```
class MyWorker
  include Sidekiq::Worker
  sidekiq_options retry: 5
```

```ruby
  def perform(*args)
    # Task logic
  end
end
```

3.3 Rate Limiting

To avoid overwhelming external services, use rate limiting for jobs.

Example: Rate-limiting API calls

ruby

```ruby
class ApiWorker
  include Sidekiq::Worker

  def perform
    sleep(1) # Pause for 1 second
    # Make API call
  end
end
```

3.4 Error Monitoring

Track job failures using monitoring tools like **Honeybadger, Sentry,** or **Sidekiq Web**.

3.5 Prioritizing Queues

Organize jobs into different queues based on priority.

Example: Configure Sidekiq queues:

yaml

```
# config/sidekiq.yml
:queues:
  - critical
  - default
  - low
```

Assign jobs to specific queues:

ruby

```
class MyWorker
  include Sidekiq::Worker
  sidekiq_options queue: 'critical'
```

end

---

4. Best Practices for Background Jobs and Task Automation

1. **Use Idempotent Jobs**: Ensure jobs can run multiple times without unintended side effects.

2. **Monitor Performance**: Use tools like **Sidekiq Web** to track job execution times and failures.

3. **Avoid Overloading the System**: Use rate limiting and prioritize critical tasks.

4. **Log Job Execution**: Log the status and output of jobs for debugging.

5. **Use Separate Queues**: Separate high-priority and low-priority jobs into different queues.

In this chapter, we explored how to handle background jobs and automate tasks in Rails. Key takeaways include:

1. Using **Active Job** for a unified interface and **Sidekiq** for high-performance job processing.

2. Scheduling recurring tasks with **Cron** and **Whenever**.

3. Efficiently managing long-running tasks with batch processing, retries, and prioritization.

By integrating these tools and techniques into your application, you can improve performance, ensure scalability, and deliver a seamless user experience.

Chapter 15: Asset Management and Deployment

Efficient asset management and a streamlined deployment process are crucial for delivering performant, scalable, and visually appealing web applications. In this chapter, we'll explore how Rails manages JavaScript, CSS, and other assets using **Webpacker**, how to precompile assets for production, and how to deploy your application to platforms like **Heroku** or other cloud services. These tools and techniques ensure that your application performs optimally in real-world scenarios.

1. Using Webpacker for JavaScript and CSS

Rails uses **Webpacker** as its default asset management tool to handle JavaScript, CSS, images, and other static files. Webpacker integrates seamlessly with Rails, providing modern JavaScript and CSS tooling via Webpack.

1.1 What is Webpacker?

Webpacker allows Rails to leverage Webpack, a JavaScript bundler that compiles modules into efficient bundles for the browser. It replaces the older asset pipeline (Sprockets) for managing modern front-end dependencies.

1.2 Setting Up Webpacker

Webpacker is included in Rails by default for applications generated with Rails 6 or later. If your application doesn't include Webpacker, you can add it manually:

1. Add Webpacker to your Gemfile:

ruby

```ruby
gem 'webpacker'
```

2. Install Webpacker:

bash

```bash
bundle install
rails webpacker:install
```

1.3 Organizing JavaScript and CSS Files

Webpacker organizes assets in the app/javascript/ directory. Common folders include:

- **packs/**: Entry points for JavaScript and CSS bundles.

- **stylesheets/**: Contains custom CSS or SCSS files.

- **images/**: Stores image assets.

1.4 Adding JavaScript Dependencies

Use Yarn, the default package manager for Rails, to add JavaScript libraries.

Example: Adding Bootstrap

1. Install Bootstrap via Yarn:

bash

```
yarn add bootstrap
```

2. Import Bootstrap in your JavaScript pack:

javascript

```
// app/javascript/packs/application.js
```

import 'bootstrap';

import '../stylesheets/application';

3. Add Bootstrap styles to the stylesheet:

scss

```
// app/javascript/stylesheets/application.scss
@import '~bootstrap/scss/bootstrap';
```

1.5 Using Webpacker Helpers in Views

Use Rails helpers to include Webpacker packs in your views.

Example: Include JavaScript and CSS packs:

erb

```
<%= javascript_pack_tag 'application', defer: true %>

<%= stylesheet_pack_tag 'application' %>
```

---

2. Precompiling Assets for Production

In development, assets are compiled on the fly, but in production, assets need to be precompiled for performance and reliability.

2.1 What is Asset Precompilation?

Precompilation is the process of bundling and minifying assets to reduce file size and improve load times. Rails automatically precompiles assets during deployment.

2.2 Precompiling Locally

To manually precompile assets, use:

bash

```
rails assets:precompile
```

This generates compiled assets in the public/assets/ directory.

2.3 Customizing the Asset Pipeline

Configure asset compilation in config/webpacker.yml. For example:

yaml

```
production:
  compile: false
  extract_css: true
```

Key options:

- **compile**: Set to false in production to use precompiled assets.

- **extract_css**: Extract CSS into separate files for production.

2.4 Managing Asset Expiry

Rails appends a hash to asset filenames to ensure browsers always load the latest version.

Example: application-123456.css

This is enabled by default but can be configured in config/environments/production.rb:

ruby

```
config.assets.digest = true
```

2.5 Debugging Asset Issues

Common asset issues include missing files or compilation errors. Use the following tips to debug:

1. Verify assets are included in the app/javascript directory.

2. Check Webpacker logs for errors:

bash

```
rails webpacker:compile
```

3. Clear old assets:

bash

```
rails assets:clobber
```

---

3. Deploying to Heroku or Cloud Services

Deployment is the process of transferring your application from the development environment to a live server. Rails is designed to work seamlessly with platforms like **Heroku** and other cloud services.

3.1 Deploying to Heroku

Heroku is a popular Platform-as-a-Service (PaaS) that simplifies deployment and scaling.

Step 1: Prerequisites

1. **Install the Heroku CLI:**

bash

```
brew tap heroku/brew && brew install heroku
```

2. **Sign Up for Heroku**: Create an account at Heroku.

Step 2: Prepare Your Application

1. **Use PostgreSQL**: Heroku requires PostgreSQL as the database. Update your Gemfile:

ruby

```
gem 'pg'
```

2. **Add a Production Environment**: Update config/database.yml:

yaml

production:

  adapter: postgresql

  encoding: unicode

  pool: 5

    3. **Add a Procfile**: Create a Procfile in the root directory:

yaml

```
web: bundle exec puma -C config/puma.rb
```

Step 3: Deploy to Heroku

    1. **Create a Heroku App**:

bash

```
heroku create my-app-name
```

    2. **Push to Heroku**:

bash

```
git push heroku main
```

3. **Run Database Migrations**:

bash

```
heroku run rails db:migrate
```

4. **Open Your App**:

bash

```
heroku open
```

3.2 Deploying to AWS, GCP, or Azure

For more control over your infrastructure, deploy to cloud platforms like AWS, Google Cloud Platform (GCP), or Microsoft Azure.

AWS Deployment

1. **Set Up Elastic Beanstalk**: Install the Elastic Beanstalk CLI:

bash

```
brew install awsebcli
```

2. **Initialize the Environment**:

```bash
```

```
eb init
```

3. **Deploy the App**:

```bash
```

```
eb deploy
```

GCP Deployment

1. **Set Up Google Cloud SDK**: Install the Google Cloud CLI:

```bash
```

```
brew install --cask google-cloud-sdk
```

2. **Deploy the App**:

```bash
```

```
gcloud app deploy
```

Azure Deployment

1. **Install Azure CLI**:

bash

brew install azure-cli

2. **Deploy the App**:

bash

az webapp up --name my-app-name

3.3 Using Docker for Deployment

Docker containers provide a consistent environment for running your Rails application across different platforms.

Example: Dockerfile for Rails

dockerfile

FROM ruby:3.1.2

WORKDIR /app

COPY Gemfile* ./

RUN bundle install

COPY . .

CMD ["rails", "server", "-b", "0.0.0.0"]

Build and run the Docker container:

bash

docker build -t my-app .

docker run -p 3000:3000 my-app

---

4. Best Practices for Asset Management and Deployment

1. **Optimize Assets**:

   o   Minimize JavaScript and CSS files.

   o   Use image compression tools.

2. **Secure Your Application**:

   o   Use HTTPS in production.

   o   Keep environment variables secure (e.g., dotenv gem).

3. **Automate Deployment**:

- o Use CI/CD pipelines for automated testing and deployment.

4. **Monitor Performance**:

   - o Use tools like New Relic or Skylight to monitor performance in production.

In this chapter, we explored the essentials of asset management and deployment. Key takeaways include:

1. **Using Webpacker**: Manage JavaScript, CSS, and other assets efficiently.

2. **Precompiling Assets**: Ensure assets are optimized for production.

3. **Deploying Applications**: Use Heroku or other cloud platforms for a streamlined deployment process.

By mastering these techniques, you can ensure your Rails application performs reliably in production, providing a seamless experience for your users.

Chapter 16: Performance Optimization

Performance optimization is a critical aspect of modern web application development, especially as your application scales and user demands grow. Optimizing a Rails application involves reducing response times, lowering resource usage, and ensuring smooth performance even under heavy traffic. This chapter explores three key areas of performance optimization: caching strategies in Rails, query optimization with eager loading, and monitoring performance in production environments.

1. Caching Strategies with Rails

Caching improves performance by storing the results of expensive operations and serving them quickly on subsequent requests. Rails provides a comprehensive caching framework that supports multiple caching techniques.

1.1 Types of Caching in Rails

1. **Page Caching**
   Entire pages are cached and served directly from the cache store, bypassing the application. This is most effective for static pages or pages that don't change frequently.

Example:

ruby

```
# config/environments/production.rb

config.action_controller.perform_caching = true

config.cache_store = :memory_store
```

Pages are saved as static files that can be served directly by the web server.

2. **Action Caching**
   Caches the output of a controller action while still processing filters and authentication. This is useful for dynamic pages that are mostly static.

Example:

ruby

```
class PostsController < ApplicationController
```

```
caches_action :index
```

```
end
```

3. **Fragment Caching**
   Caches specific parts of a view, such as headers, footers, or frequently rendered data.

Example:

erb

```
<% cache @post do %>

 <%= render @post %>

<% end %>
```

4. **Low-Level Caching**
   Directly stores arbitrary data in the cache store, independent of controllers or views.

Example:

ruby

```
Rails.cache.fetch('expensive_operation', expires_in:
12.hours) do

 perform_expensive_operation

end
```

1.2 Choosing a Cache Store

Rails supports multiple cache stores. Common options include:

- **MemoryStore**: Stores data in memory (best for development).

- **FileStore**: Stores cache files on disk.

- **Redis**: A popular in-memory key-value store for production use.

- **Memcached**: Another high-performance caching solution.

Configure the cache store in config/environments/production.rb:

ruby

```ruby
config.cache_store = :redis_cache_store, { url: 'redis://localhost:6379/0' }
```

1.3 Expiring Cached Data

Cached data should be invalidated or expired when it becomes outdated.

Example: Expire fragment caches:

ruby

expire_fragment(@post)

Use touch to update the cache key automatically when a model is updated:

ruby

```ruby
class Post < ApplicationRecord
  has_many :comments, touch: true
end
```

1.4 View-Level Caching Best Practices

1. **Cache Expensive Partial Renders**:

erb

```erb
<% cache 'recent_posts' do %>
  <%= render @recent_posts %>
<% end %>
```

2. **Use Conditional Caching**: Only cache if certain conditions are met.

erb

```
<% cache @user if @user.premium? do %>
  <%= render @user %>
<% end %>
```

3. **Compress Cached Content**: Compress cached HTML or data to reduce file size.

---

2. Query Optimization and Eager Loading

Inefficient database queries are a common performance bottleneck. Optimizing Active Record queries and using techniques like eager loading can significantly reduce query execution time.

2.1 Understanding the N+1 Query Problem

The N+1 query problem occurs when a query fetches records one by one instead of using a single, optimized query.

Example: Problematic query:

ruby

```
@posts = Post.all

@posts.each do |post|

  puts post.comments.count

end
```

This generates one query for @posts and an additional query for each post's comments.

2.2 Solving N+1 with Eager Loading

Eager loading fetches associated records in a single query using includes or joins.

Example: Using includes:

ruby

```
@posts = Post.includes(:comments)

@posts.each do |post|

  puts post.comments.count

end
```

This generates a single query for posts and their associated comments.

2.3 Using joins for Advanced Queries

joins is used to combine data from multiple tables, ideal for filtering or sorting by associated records.

Example: Filter posts by comment content:

ruby

```
@posts = Post.joins(:comments).where(comments: { content: 'Great post!' })
```

2.4 Batch Processing Large Datasets

Use batch processing methods like find_each to process large datasets efficiently.

Example:

ruby

```
Post.find_each(batch_size: 100) do |post|
  puts post.title
end
```

2.5 Indexing for Faster Queries

Database indexes speed up query performance by reducing lookup time. Add indexes to frequently queried columns.

Migration example:

bash

```
rails generate migration AddIndexToPostsTitle
```

Migration file:

ruby

```
class AddIndexToPostsTitle <
ActiveRecord::Migration[6.1]
  def change
    add_index :posts, :title
  end
end
```

2.6 Optimizing Query Performance

1. **Select Specific Columns**: Fetch only the required columns instead of entire records.

ruby

```
Post.select(:id, :title)
```

2. **Avoid Unnecessary Queries**: Use exists? to check for record existence.

ruby

```
Post.exists?(title: 'Example')
```

3. **Defer Complex Operations**: Use raw SQL for complex queries.

ruby

```
Post.find_by_sql("SELECT * FROM posts WHERE published = true")
```

---

3. Monitoring Performance in Production

Monitoring tools provide insights into how your application performs in real-world scenarios, helping you identify bottlenecks and optimize critical paths.

3.1 Performance Monitoring Tools

1. **New Relic**: Tracks response times, database queries, and error rates in real-time.

   o Installation:

bash

```
bundle add newrelic_rpm
```

2. **Skylight**: Focuses on identifying slow parts of your application.

   o Installation:

bash

```
gem 'skylight'
```

3. **Scout**: A lightweight performance monitoring tool.

   o Installation:

bash

```
gem 'scout_apm'
```

3.2 Logging Performance Metrics

Use Rails logs to measure performance. Enable query logs in config/environments/production.rb:

ruby

```
config.active_record.verbose_query_logs = true
```

3.3 Profiling with Rack Mini Profiler

Rack Mini Profiler provides real-time performance insights for your development environment.

Installation:

bash

```
gem 'rack-mini-profiler'
```

Usage:

ruby

```
Rack::MiniProfiler.authorize_request
```

3.4 Measuring Database Performance

Use Active Record query logs to identify slow queries. Slow query example:

bash

Processing by PostsController#index

 Post Load (200.1ms) SELECT * FROM "posts"

Optimize slow queries using indexes, eager loading, or query restructuring.

3.5 Setting Up Alerts for Production

Configure alerts to notify you of performance degradation.

Example: New Relic Alerts

1. Set thresholds for response times and error rates.

2. Configure email or Slack notifications.

---

4. Best Practices for Performance Optimization

1. **Measure Before Optimizing**: Use tools to identify bottlenecks before attempting optimizations.

2. **Leverage Caching**: Cache frequently accessed data to reduce load times.

3. **Use Eager Loading**: Always use includes to avoid N+1 query problems.

4. **Monitor Regularly**: Continuously monitor production performance to identify issues early.

5. **Optimize Database Structure**: Regularly analyze and index critical database columns.

Performance optimization is a continuous process that evolves as your application grows. In this chapter, we covered:

1. **Caching Strategies**: Using Rails caching mechanisms to improve response times.

2. **Query Optimization**: Avoiding N+1 problems, indexing, and optimizing database queries.

3. **Monitoring Tools**: Tracking performance metrics in production using tools like New Relic and Skylight.

By applying these techniques, you can ensure your Rails application is fast, efficient, and scalable, delivering a seamless user experience even under high demand.

Chapter 17: Real-Time Features with ActionCable

Real-time features have become a cornerstone of modern web applications, enabling dynamic interactions like live chats, notifications, and collaborative tools. Rails provides **ActionCable**, a powerful library for integrating **WebSockets** into your application. This chapter covers the fundamentals of WebSockets, how to use ActionCable to build real-time features like chat and notification systems, and techniques for scaling these features to handle large traffic efficiently.

1. Introduction to WebSockets

1.1 What Are WebSockets?

WebSockets provide a persistent, full-duplex communication channel between a client and a server over a single TCP connection. Unlike HTTP, which requires repeated requests for data,

WebSockets enable the server to send updates to the client instantly.

1.2 Advantages of WebSockets

1. **Real-Time Communication**: Instant updates without polling.

2. **Reduced Overhead**: Single connection reduces the need for multiple HTTP requests.

3. **Scalability**: Ideal for applications requiring frequent updates, such as live notifications.

1.3 WebSockets in Rails with ActionCable

Rails' ActionCable integrates WebSockets into the Rails ecosystem, allowing seamless real-time features alongside traditional HTTP interactions.

Key Features:

- Built-in WebSocket support.

- Tightly integrated with Rails' models, controllers, and views.

- Easy to scale using Redis or other backends.

2. Building Real-Time Features with ActionCable

2.1 Setting Up ActionCable

ActionCable is included by default in Rails. Follow these steps to set up a basic ActionCable configuration:

1. **Enable ActionCable**: Ensure the ActionCable gem is included in your Rails application.

2. **Configure Cable**: Open config/cable.yml to set the development and production environments:

yaml

development:

  adapter: async

production:

  adapter: redis

  url: redis://localhost:6379/1

3. **Mount ActionCable**: Mount ActionCable in your config/routes.rb file:

ruby

```ruby
mount ActionCable.server => '/cable'
```

2.2 Creating a Channel

A **channel** is the foundation of ActionCable and represents a WebSocket connection. For example, to create a channel for chat:

Generate the channel:

bash

```bash
rails generate channel Chat
```

This creates:

1. **Channel File**:
   app/channels/chat_channel.rb:

ruby

```ruby
class ChatChannel < ApplicationCable::Channel
  def subscribed
    stream_from "chat_channel"
  end
```

```ruby
def unsubscribed
  # Any cleanup needed when channel is
unsubscribed
end


def speak(data)
  ActionCable.server.broadcast("chat_channel",
message: data["message"])
end
end
```

2. **JavaScript File**:
   app/javascript/channels/chat_channel.js:

javascript

```javascript
import consumer from "./consumer";


consumer.subscriptions.create("ChatChannel", {
 connected() {
  console.log("Connected to ChatChannel");
 },
```

```
disconnected() {

  console.log("Disconnected from ChatChannel");

},

received(data) {

  console.log("Received:", data);

},

speak(message) {

  this.perform("speak", { message });

},

});
```

2.3 Broadcasting Messages

Broadcasting allows the server to send messages to all subscribed clients. In Rails, you can broadcast messages using:

ruby

```ruby
ActionCable.server.broadcast("chat_channel",
message: "Hello, World!")
```

2.4 Building a Live Chat System

Let's create a real-time chat application using ActionCable.

Step 1: Define the Chat Model

Generate a model for chat messages:

bash

```
rails generate model Message content:string
rails db:migrate
```

Add an association:

ruby

```ruby
class Message < ApplicationRecord
  validates :content, presence: true
end
```

Step 2: Update the Channel

Modify the ChatChannel to stream messages:

ruby

```ruby
class ChatChannel < ApplicationCable::Channel
  def subscribed
    stream_from "chat_channel"
  end

  def speak(data)
    Message.create!(content: data["message"])
    ActionCable.server.broadcast("chat_channel",
message: data["message"])
  end
end
```

Step 3: Frontend JavaScript

Update the chat_channel.js file to append messages to the chat:

javascript

```javascript
import consumer from "./consumer";

consumer.subscriptions.create("ChatChannel", {
```

```
received(data) {

  const messages =
document.getElementById("messages");

  messages.insertAdjacentHTML("beforeend",
`<p>${data.message}</p>`);

 },

 speak(message) {

  this.perform("speak", { message });

 },

});


// Trigger the "speak" method when the user sends
a message

document.getElementById("chat-
form").addEventListener("submit", function (e) {

  e.preventDefault();

  const messageInput =
document.getElementById("message-input");


consumer.subscriptions.subscriptions[0].speak(m
essageInput.value);

  messageInput.value = "";
```

```
});
```

Step 4: Add the Chat View

Add a simple chat interface in your view:

erb

```
<div id="messages"></div>

<form id="chat-form">

  <input type="text" id="message-input"
placeholder="Type a message...">

  <button type="submit">Send</button>

</form>
```

2.5 Real-Time Notifications

Notifications are another common use case for ActionCable. Implement a notification system by broadcasting alerts to users when certain events occur.

Example:

1. Broadcast a notification:

ruby

```
ActionCable.server.broadcast("notifications_#{user
.id}", alert: "New message received!")
```

2. Update the client-side JavaScript:

javascript

```
consumer.subscriptions.create({ channel:
"NotificationsChannel", user_id: userId }, {

  received(data) {

    alert(data.alert);

  },

});
```

3. Scaling Real-Time Features

Real-time features like chat and notifications require careful consideration to scale effectively under high traffic.

3.1 Using Redis for Scaling

Redis is a high-performance in-memory database and message broker that ActionCable uses in production to handle connections and broadcasts.

Setting Up Redis

Install Redis on your server or use a managed service like AWS Elasticache.

Update config/cable.yml for production:

yaml

```
production:
 adapter: redis
 url: redis://your-redis-server:6379/1
 channel_prefix: my_app_production
```

3.2 Load Balancing WebSocket Connections

For large-scale applications, use a load balancer to distribute WebSocket connections across multiple servers.

Setting Up a Load Balancer

1. Use Nginx or AWS ELB to distribute traffic.

2. Configure sticky sessions to ensure a client maintains a connection to the same server.

Example Nginx configuration:

nginx

```
upstream websocket_backend {
  server app1.example.com;
  server app2.example.com;
}

server {
  location /cable {
    proxy_pass http://websocket_backend;
    proxy_http_version 1.1;
    proxy_set_header Upgrade $http_upgrade;
    proxy_set_header Connection "Upgrade";
    proxy_set_header Host $host;
  }
}
```

3.3 Monitoring and Debugging WebSockets

Use tools like **CableReady** or **AnyCable** to monitor WebSocket connections and ensure they remain stable under load.

1. **CableReady**: Provides advanced debugging tools for ActionCable.

2. **AnyCable**: Replaces ActionCable with a more efficient WebSocket server.

3.4 Optimizing Performance

1. **Minimize Payloads**: Send only necessary data in WebSocket messages.

ruby

```ruby
ActionCable.server.broadcast("chat_channel", message: message.content)
```

2. **Close Idle Connections**: Automatically close connections that remain idle for a specified period.

3. **Use Horizontal Scaling**: Add more WebSocket servers as traffic increases.

4. Best Practices for Real-Time Features

1. **Security**:

    o Authenticate users before subscribing to a channel.

    o Use unique channel identifiers (e.g., notifications_#{user.id}) to prevent unauthorized access.

2. **Performance**:

    o Use Redis for production.

    o Avoid excessive broadcasting by targeting specific channels.

3. **Scalability**:

    o Use sticky sessions for WebSocket connections.

    o Scale horizontally with load balancers.

4. **Testing**:

    o Test real-time features under simulated high traffic.

    o Verify connection stability and message delivery.

In this chapter, we explored how to integrate real-time features into Rails applications using ActionCable. Key takeaways include:

1. **Understanding WebSockets**: Persistent, full-duplex communication for real-time updates.

2. **Building Features with ActionCable**: Creating live chat and notification systems.

3. **Scaling Real-Time Features**: Using Redis, load balancers, and performance optimizations to handle high traffic.

By mastering these techniques, you can build dynamic, real-time Rails applications that deliver exceptional user experiences, even under demanding conditions.

Chapter 18: Localization and Internationalization

In today's globalized world, applications often serve users across different languages and regions. **Internationalization (I18n)** and **Localization (L10n)** in Rails empower developers to adapt applications for multilingual audiences. **Internationalization** refers to the process of designing an application so it can be adapted to different languages and regions without changes to its source code, while **localization** involves translating and formatting data to suit a specific locale.

This chapter explores how to set up I18n in Rails, manage translation files, and follow best practices for multi-language support, enabling your application to reach a broader audience.

1. Setting Up I18n in Rails

Rails includes robust support for I18n out of the box, making it easy to create applications that can support multiple languages and locales.

1.1 What is I18n?

The term **I18n** (short for internationalization) refers to adapting software for different languages and cultures. Rails uses the I18n gem to manage translations and locale-specific content.

1.2 Configuring I18n

The default locale in Rails is English (en). You can set the default or change the locale dynamically.

1. **Set the Default Locale**: Update the default locale in config/application.rb:

ruby

```
module MyApp

 class Application < Rails::Application

  config.i18n.default_locale = :en

 end

end
```

2. **Add Additional Locales**: Rails supports multiple locales. To add support for another

language (e.g., French), create a translation file:

yaml

```
# config/locales/fr.yml

fr:

 hello: "Bonjour"
```

3. **Change the Locale Dynamically**: Use a before_action in your application controller:

ruby

```
class ApplicationController <
ActionController::Base

 before_action :set_locale


 private


 def set_locale

  I18n.locale = params[:locale] ||
I18n.default_locale
 end
```

end

Pass the locale parameter in URLs:

erb

```erb
<%= link_to "French", root_path(locale: :fr) %>
```

1.3 Fallbacks for Missing Translations

When translations for a specific locale are missing, Rails can fallback to the default locale. Enable fallbacks in config/application.rb:

ruby

```ruby
config.i18n.fallbacks = true
```

2. Managing Translation Files

Translation files are YAML files that define locale-specific translations for your application. Proper organization and management of these files are crucial for maintaining scalability and readability.

2.1 Structure of Translation Files

Translation files are structured as a nested hierarchy of keys and values. The top-level key corresponds to the locale (e.g., en or fr).

Example: config/locales/en.yml

yaml

```
en:
  hello: "Hello"
  navigation:
    home: "Home"
    about: "About Us"
```

Example: config/locales/fr.yml

yaml

```
fr:
  hello: "Bonjour"
  navigation:
    home: "Accueil"
    about: "À propos"
```

2.2 Interpolating Variables in Translations

Rails allows you to insert dynamic content into translations using placeholders.

Example:

yaml

en:

  greeting: "Hello, %{name}!"

In your view or controller:

ruby

t('greeting', name: 'Alice') # Outputs: "Hello, Alice!"

2.3 Pluralization

Rails supports pluralization for languages with singular and plural forms.

Example:

yaml

en:

  car:

one: "1 car"

other: "%{count} cars"

Usage:

ruby

t('car', count: 1) # Outputs: "1 car"

t('car', count: 5) # Outputs: "5 cars"

2.4 Handling Complex Pluralization Rules

Some languages have more complex pluralization rules. Rails allows you to define these rules in a custom backend or use the i18n gem's pluralization support.

2.5 Organizing Translation Files

For large applications, organize translation files into multiple smaller files to improve maintainability.

Example Directory Structure:

arduino

config/locales/

en.yml

fr.yml

views/

  en/

    posts.yml

    comments.yml

  fr/

    posts.yml

    comments.yml

2.6 Testing Translations

To ensure translations are complete and accurate, use gems like **i18n-tasks**.

Installation:

bash

gem install i18n-tasks

Check for missing translations:

bash

i18n-tasks missing

3. Best Practices for Multi-Language Support

Implementing multi-language support in Rails requires thoughtful design to ensure maintainability, performance, and a seamless user experience.

3.1 Keep Keys Descriptive

Use descriptive keys for translations to make files self-explanatory.

Example:

yaml

```
en:
  navigation:
    home: "Home"
    about: "About Us"
```

3.2 Avoid Hardcoding Strings

Never hardcode strings directly in your views or controllers. Use the t helper for translations.

Example:

erb

```
<%= t('navigation.home') %> <!-- Outputs: "Home" -->
```

3.3 Use Helpers for Repeated Translations

For repeated translations, define helper methods to simplify code.

Example:

ruby

```
module ApplicationHelper
  def localized_date(date)
    l(date, format: :long)
  end
end
```

3.4 Support Right-to-Left Languages

For languages like Arabic or Hebrew, ensure your application supports **right-to-left (RTL)** layouts. Add a dir attribute dynamically based on the locale.

Example:

html

```
<html lang="<%= I18n.locale %>" dir="<%= I18n.locale == :ar ? 'rtl' : 'ltr' %>">
```

3.5 Use Locale-Specific Assets

Serve locale-specific assets (e.g., images or PDFs) when necessary.

Example:

erb

```
<%= image_tag "logo_#{I18n.locale}.png" %>
```

3.6 Test Multi-Language Features

1. **Test with All Supported Locales**: Ensure the application works correctly in each locale.

2. **Simulate Real-World Scenarios**: Test with large strings, special characters, and different formats.

3. **Automate Localization Tests**: Use tools like **RSpec** to automate tests for translated content.

3.7 Handle Date, Time, and Number Formats

Localization extends beyond text to include dates, times, and numbers. Rails provides tools to format these values based on the locale.

Example:

yaml

```yaml
en:
  date:
    formats:
      default: "%Y-%m-%d"
fr:
  date:
    formats:
      default: "%d/%m/%Y"
```

Usage:

ruby

l(Date.today, format: :default) # Outputs date in the current locale format

---

3.8 Fallbacks for Missing Translations

Always define fallbacks for locales with incomplete translations to avoid runtime errors. This ensures the application continues to function even if some translations are missing.

---

4. Advanced Localization Features

Rails provides advanced localization features to handle complex requirements.

4.1 Localizing Routes

You can localize routes to provide a seamless experience for users in different regions.

Example:

ruby

```ruby
scope "(:locale)", locale: /en|fr/ do
  resources :posts
end
```

Generate localized URLs:

erb

```erb
<%= link_to t('navigation.home'), root_path(locale: :fr) %>
```

4.2 Localized Views

Serve locale-specific views by creating separate templates for each language.

Example Directory Structure:

bash

```bash
app/views/posts/index.html.erb    # Default view

app/views/posts/index.fr.html.erb   # French view
```

Rails automatically serves the localized template based on the current locale.

4.3 Custom I18n Backends

For advanced use cases, create a custom I18n backend. For example, fetch translations from a database instead of YAML files.

Example:

ruby

```
I18n.backend = I18n::Backend::ActiveRecord.new
```

5. Challenges in Multi-Language Support

1. **Handling Complex Grammars**: Some languages require context-specific translations, which can complicate implementation.

2. **Maintaining Consistency**: Ensuring translations stay updated as the application evolves requires regular audits.

3. **Performance Considerations**: Large translation files can increase memory usage. Use lazy loading or custom backends to improve performance.

6. Real-World Applications of I18n

1. **E-Commerce**: Display product descriptions, prices, and currencies in the user's language and locale.

2. **Content Platforms**: Deliver articles or blogs in the preferred language of the user.

3. **SaaS Applications**: Enable global users to interact with the software in their native language, increasing accessibility.

Localization and internationalization are essential for building Rails applications that cater to a global audience. In this chapter, we covered:

1. **Setting Up I18n**: Configuring Rails for multi-language support.

2. **Managing Translation Files**: Organizing, interpolating, and testing translations.

3. **Best Practices**: Ensuring maintainability, performance, and usability in multi-language applications.

By following these practices and leveraging Rails' powerful I18n tools, you can create applications that provide seamless experiences for users across different languages and regions.

Chapter 19: Securing Your Rails Applications

Web application security is critical for protecting sensitive user data and ensuring system integrity. Ruby on Rails provides robust tools and configurations to mitigate vulnerabilities, but developers must implement best practices to safeguard applications from attacks. This chapter explores common vulnerabilities like SQL injection and Cross-Site Request Forgery (CSRF), securing applications with HTTPS and secure headers, and managing environment variables securely.

1. Protecting Against Common Vulnerabilities

Modern web applications are exposed to various security threats. Rails includes built-in protections against many of these vulnerabilities, but understanding their mechanisms is essential.

1.1 SQL Injection

SQL injection occurs when an attacker manipulates SQL queries by injecting malicious input, potentially exposing or modifying database data.

Example of SQL Injection:

ruby

```
# Vulnerable Code

Post.where("title = '#{params[:title]}'")
```

If a malicious user submits '; DROP TABLE posts;--, the query becomes:

sql

```
SELECT * FROM posts WHERE title = ''; DROP TABLE posts;--
```

Preventing SQL Injection

Rails' **Active Record** uses parameterized queries to prevent SQL injection. Always pass user input as parameters:

ruby

```
# Safe Code

Post.where(title: params[:title])
```

Use sanitize_sql for custom queries:

ruby

```ruby
sanitized_query =
ActiveRecord::Base.sanitize_sql(["title = ?",
params[:title]])

Post.where(sanitized_query)
```

1.2 Cross-Site Request Forgery (CSRF)

CSRF attacks trick authenticated users into performing unintended actions on your application.

Rails' Built-In CSRF Protection

Rails includes CSRF protection by default. It uses a unique token embedded in forms and verified on the server.

Example:

erb

```erb
<%= form_with model: @post do |form| %>
  <%= form.text_field :title %>
  <%= form.submit %>
```

```
<% end %>
```

The token is automatically added as a hidden field:

html

```html
<input type="hidden" name="authenticity_token" value="abc123">
```

Verifying CSRF Tokens

The server verifies the token to ensure the request originates from the same application:

ruby

```ruby
class ApplicationController < ActionController::Base
  protect_from_forgery with: :exception
end
```

If you need to disable CSRF for specific actions (e.g., APIs), use:

ruby

```ruby
skip_forgery_protection
```

1.3 Cross-Site Scripting (XSS)

XSS attacks occur when malicious scripts are injected into web pages, often through user inputs.

Example of XSS:

erb

```
<%= params[:name] %>
```

If a user submits <script>alert('Hacked');</script>, the browser executes the script.

Preventing XSS

Rails automatically escapes outputs in views:

erb

```
<%= params[:name] %> <!-- Escaped Output -->
```

For safe raw output, use:

erb

```
<%= raw(params[:name]) %>
```

1.4 Mass Assignment Vulnerabilities

Mass assignment occurs when attackers exploit unprotected model attributes to inject malicious data.

Example:

ruby

```
# Vulnerable Code
User.new(params[:user])
```

If a user submits:

json

```
{ "admin": true }
```

An unintended admin user may be created.

Preventing Mass Assignment

Use **Strong Parameters** to whitelist allowed attributes:

ruby

```ruby
def user_params
  params.require(:user).permit(:name, :email)
end


User.new(user_params)
```

1.5 Authentication Vulnerabilities

Authentication vulnerabilities, like weak passwords or session hijacking, compromise user accounts.

Best Practices:

1. **Use Secure Authentication Gems**: Use gems like **Devise** to handle authentication securely.

2. **Hash Passwords**: Use Rails' has_secure_password for hashing passwords with bcrypt:

ruby

```ruby
class User < ApplicationRecord
  has_secure_password
```

end

3. **Implement Multi-Factor Authentication (MFA)**: Add an additional layer of security using gems like **authy** or **devise-two-factor**.

---

2. Using Secure Headers and HTTPS

2.1 Secure Headers

Secure headers instruct browsers on how to handle content, reducing vulnerabilities like XSS and Clickjacking.

Setting Secure Headers

Rails includes the **SecureHeaders** gem. Install it:

bash

```
gem install secure_headers
```

Add default security headers in config/initializers/secure_headers.rb:

ruby

```
SecureHeaders::Configuration.default do |config|
```

```ruby
config.x_frame_options = "DENY"

config.x_content_type_options = "nosniff"

config.x_xss_protection = "1; mode=block"

config.content_security_policy = {

  default_src: ["'self'"],

  script_src: ["'self'", "https://trusted-scripts.example.com"],

  style_src: ["'self'", "https://trusted-styles.example.com"]

 }
end
```

Content Security Policy (CSP)

CSP prevents the browser from loading untrusted resources:

ruby

```ruby
Rails.application.config.content_security_policy do |policy|

  policy.default_src :self

  policy.script_src :self, :https
```

```ruby
policy.style_src :self, :https
```

```ruby
end
```

2.2 Enforcing HTTPS

HTTPS encrypts data between the browser and server, protecting sensitive information.

Enabling HTTPS in Rails

1. Force HTTPS in production:

ruby

```ruby
config.force_ssl = true
```

2. Redirect HTTP requests to HTTPS using a reverse proxy or web server configuration (e.g., Nginx).

3. Obtain an SSL certificate using services like **Let's Encrypt**.

HSTS (HTTP Strict Transport Security)

HSTS forces browsers to use HTTPS for all subsequent requests:

ruby

```ruby
config.ssl_options = { hsts: { expires: 1.year,
subdomains: true } }
```

2.3 Securing Cookies

1. **Mark Cookies as Secure**: Only transmit cookies over HTTPS:

ruby

```ruby
cookies[:user_id] = { value: user.id, secure:
Rails.env.production? }
```

2. **Use HttpOnly Cookies**: Prevent JavaScript from accessing cookies:

ruby

```ruby
cookies[:session] = { value: session_id, httponly:
true }
```

---

3. Configuring Environment Variables Securely

3.1 Why Secure Environment Variables?

Environment variables often store sensitive data, such as API keys, database credentials, or encryption secrets. Exposing these variables can lead to significant security breaches.

3.2 Using the Rails Credentials System

Rails provides an encrypted credentials store for sensitive data.

Setting Up Credentials

Generate credentials:

bash

```
rails credentials:edit
```

This opens an editor to add key-value pairs:

yaml

```
aws:

  access_key_id: "your-access-key"

  secret_access_key: "your-secret-key"
```

Access credentials in code:

ruby

```
Rails.application.credentials.aws[:access_key_id]
```

3.3 Using Environment Variables

For simpler configurations, use environment variables. Rails provides the **dotenv** gem to manage them.

Installing Dotenv

Add to your Gemfile:

ruby

```
gem 'dotenv-rails', groups: [:development, :test]
```

Create a .env file:

env

```
DATABASE_URL=postgres://user:password@localh
ost/mydb
```

```
SECRET_KEY_BASE=your-secret-key
```

Load variables in Rails:

ruby

```
ENV['DATABASE_URL']
```

3.4 Avoid Committing Sensitive Data

1. Add sensitive files like .env to .gitignore:

gitignore

```
.env
```

```
config/credentials.yml.enc
```

2. Use secrets management tools like **AWS Secrets Manager** or **HashiCorp Vault** for production.

4. Best Practices for Securing Rails Applications

1. **Keep Gems Updated**: Regularly update gems to patch security vulnerabilities:

bash

```
bundle update
```

2. **Use Strong Passwords**: Enforce password complexity using Devise or custom validations.

3. **Audit Logs**: Log access and actions to detect suspicious activity.

4. **Implement Rate Limiting**: Prevent brute force attacks by limiting login attempts using gems like **rack-attack.**

5. **Run Security Scanners**: Use tools like **Brakeman** for static code analysis:

bash

```
gem install brakeman
brakeman
```

6. **Secure File Uploads**: Use gems like **CarrierWave** or **ActiveStorage** with validations to prevent malicious uploads.

7. **Use Read-Only Database Accounts**: Restrict database access for web applications to read-only for sensitive tables.

8. **Test Security**: Perform penetration testing to identify vulnerabilities.

Securing a Rails application involves protecting against common vulnerabilities, enforcing secure communication, and safeguarding sensitive data. In this chapter, you learned:

1. **How to Prevent Common Vulnerabilities**: Mitigate SQL injection, XSS, and CSRF attacks.

2. **Implement Secure Headers and HTTPS**: Use CSP, secure cookies, and encrypted connections.

3. **Manage Environment Variables Securely**: Use Rails credentials and environment variables without exposing sensitive data.

By implementing these best practices, you can ensure that your Rails application remains secure, reliable, and trustworthy for users.

Chapter 20: Scaling Rails Applications

As your Rails application grows in user base and complexity, it must handle increased traffic, larger datasets, and higher concurrency efficiently. Scaling a Rails application involves both architectural changes and performance optimizations. This chapter explores the fundamentals of **vertical and horizontal scaling**, techniques for optimizing Rails applications for high traffic, and an introduction to using **Docker for containerization** to ensure scalability and reliability.

1. Vertical and Horizontal Scaling Approaches

Scaling strategies can be broadly classified into **vertical scaling** and **horizontal scaling**.

1.1 Vertical Scaling

Vertical scaling involves increasing the resources of a single server to handle more load. This may include upgrading hardware such as CPU, RAM, and storage.

Advantages of Vertical Scaling

1. **Simplicity**: Easier to implement as it requires no architectural changes.

2. **Single Point of Management**: Reduces complexity by managing only one server.

Disadvantages of Vertical Scaling

1. **Resource Limits**: There's a finite limit to how much hardware can be upgraded.

2. **Downtime**: Upgrades often require shutting down the server.

Use Case for Vertical Scaling

Vertical scaling is ideal for small to medium-sized applications where traffic growth is predictable.

1.2 Horizontal Scaling

Horizontal scaling distributes the load across multiple servers. Instead of upgrading one server, you add more servers to handle the workload.

Advantages of Horizontal Scaling

1. **Infinite Scalability**: Add servers as demand grows.

2. **Fault Tolerance**: If one server fails, others can continue serving traffic.

3. **Cost Efficiency**: Use commodity hardware instead of investing in expensive upgrades.

Disadvantages of Horizontal Scaling

1. **Complexity**: Requires load balancers and distributed systems.

2. **Consistency Issues**: Data synchronization across servers can be challenging.

Use Case for Horizontal Scaling

Horizontal scaling is suitable for large-scale applications that experience sudden spikes in traffic.

Implementing Horizontal Scaling

1. **Load Balancers**: Tools like **NGINX, HAProxy,** or **AWS ELB** distribute traffic across servers.

2. **Database Replication**: Use primary-replica setups for databases to balance read/write loads.

3. **Caching Layers**: Introduce caching with **Redis** or **Memcached** to reduce database load.

---

2. Optimizing for High Traffic and Concurrency

Rails applications must be optimized to handle high traffic and concurrent user requests without degrading performance.

2.1 Using a Reverse Proxy

A reverse proxy improves performance and scalability by handling incoming requests before they reach the Rails server.

Popular Reverse Proxies

1. **NGINX**: Configures as a reverse proxy and load balancer. Example:

nginx

```
server {

  listen 80;

  server_name example.com;


  location / {

    proxy_pass http://localhost:3000;

    proxy_set_header Host $host;

    proxy_set_header X-Real-IP $remote_addr;

  }

}
```

2. **Apache**: Alternative to NGINX for serving Rails applications.

2.2 Database Optimization

Efficient database management is crucial for scaling.

Techniques for Database Optimization:

1. **Indexing**: Add indexes to frequently queried columns.

ruby

```
add_index :users, :email
```

2. **Query Optimization**: Use includes or joins to avoid N+1 query problems.

3. **Database Sharding**: Split data across multiple databases to reduce load.

4. **Read Replicas**: Use read replicas to distribute read operations.

2.3 Caching

Caching stores frequently accessed data in memory to reduce database and server load.

Types of Caching in Rails:

1. **Fragment Caching**: Cache parts of views using cache blocks.

erb

```erb
<% cache @post do %>
 <%= render @post %>
<% end %>
```

2. **Low-Level Caching**: Cache arbitrary data with Rails.cache.

ruby

```
Rails.cache.fetch("key") { expensive_operation }
```

3. **HTTP Caching**: Use browser caching and ETags to reduce redundant requests.

2.4 Background Jobs

Move long-running tasks to background jobs to free up server resources.

Tools for Background Jobs:

1. **Sidekiq**: High-performance job processing using Redis.

2. **Delayed Job**: Queues tasks directly in the database.

3. **Resque**: Redis-based background job processor.

2.5 Concurrent Web Servers

Rails applications use web servers like **Puma** or **Unicorn** to handle requests. Configure these servers to improve concurrency.

Example: Configuring Puma

config/puma.rb:

ruby

```
threads_count =
ENV.fetch("RAILS_MAX_THREADS") { 5 }.to_i

threads threads_count, threads_count

workers ENV.fetch("WEB_CONCURRENCY") { 2 }

preload_app!
```

2.6 Scaling Application Logic

1. **Service Objects**: Move complex logic to service objects for modular code.

2. **Microservices**: Split large applications into smaller, independent services.

---

3. Introduction to Containerization with Docker

Containerization is a modern approach to deploying scalable applications. Containers encapsulate applications and their dependencies, ensuring consistency across environments.

3.1 What is Docker?

Docker is a containerization platform that packages applications and their dependencies into portable containers.

Benefits of Docker:

1. **Environment Consistency**: Identical development, staging, and production environments.

2. **Scalability**: Easily scale containers horizontally.

3. **Portability**: Containers run anywhere Docker is installed.

3.2 Setting Up Docker for Rails

Step 1: Install Docker

Install Docker Desktop on your local machine or server.

Step 2: Create a Dockerfile

A Dockerfile defines the application environment.

Example:

dockerfile

FROM ruby:3.1.2

WORKDIR /app

Install dependencies

COPY Gemfile* ./

RUN bundle install

Add application files

```
COPY . .
```

```
# Precompile assets
RUN bundle exec rake assets:precompile
```

```
# Expose the port
EXPOSE 3000
```

```
# Start the server
CMD ["rails", "server", "-b", "0.0.0.0"]
```

Step 3: Build the Docker Image

bash

```bash
docker build -t my-rails-app .
```

Step 4: Run the Container

bash

```bash
docker run -p 3000:3000 my-rails-app
```

3.3 Using Docker Compose

Docker Compose manages multi-container applications. For example, a Rails application might require containers for the app server, database, and Redis.

Example: docker-compose.yml

yaml

```yaml
version: '3.9'
services:
  app:
    build:
      context: .
    ports:
      - "3000:3000"
    volumes:
      - ".:/app"
    depends_on:
      - db
```

```yaml
    - redis
  db:
    image: postgres
    environment:
      POSTGRES_USER: user
      POSTGRES_PASSWORD: password
  redis:
    image: redis
```

Run the application:

bash

```bash
docker-compose up
```

3.4 Scaling with Docker Swarm or Kubernetes

Use orchestration tools like Docker Swarm or Kubernetes to scale containers across multiple servers.

Kubernetes Overview:

1. Define application configurations in **YAML** files.

2. Use Kubernetes clusters to manage deployments and scaling.

3. Monitor container performance with tools like Prometheus and Grafana.

---

4. Best Practices for Scaling Rails Applications

4.1 Monitor Application Performance

1. Use tools like **New Relic**, **Skylight**, or **Scout** to monitor response times, error rates, and server load.

2. Track database query performance with **pgHero**.

4.2 Automate Scaling

1. Use auto-scaling groups in cloud platforms (e.g., AWS Auto Scaling, Google Cloud Instance Groups).

2. Configure load balancers to add or remove servers dynamically.

4.3 Optimize Code and Architecture

1. Reduce response times by optimizing Rails controllers and queries.

2. Break monolithic applications into microservices.

4.4 Plan for Downtime

1. Use rolling updates to minimize downtime during deployments.

2. Set up failover servers and disaster recovery mechanisms.

4.5 Secure Your Application

1. Use environment variables to store secrets and credentials.

2. Encrypt sensitive data and enforce HTTPS across all connections.

Scaling a Rails application requires a combination of infrastructure enhancements, performance optimizations, and modern deployment techniques. In this chapter, we covered:

1. **Vertical and Horizontal Scaling**: Understanding when and how to scale servers.

2. **Optimizing for High Traffic**: Techniques like caching, load balancing, and concurrent processing.

3. **Containerization with Docker**: Using Docker and orchestration tools like Kubernetes for scalable, consistent deployments.

By adopting these strategies, you can ensure that your Rails application remains responsive, reliable, and capable of handling growing user demands.

Chapter 21: Hands-On Project: Building a Blog Platform

Building a blog platform is a practical way to apply your Rails knowledge. This project involves planning and wireframing the application, implementing core features like user accounts, posts, and comments, and deploying the final project to production. By the end of this chapter, you'll have a fully functional blog application that demonstrates the core concepts of Ruby on Rails.

1. Planning and Wireframing the App

1.1 Defining Requirements

Before diving into development, define the application's core features:

1. **User Authentication**: Allow users to sign up, log in, and manage their accounts.

2. **Posts**: Users can create, edit, and delete blog posts.

3. **Comments**: Readers can comment on posts.

4. **Admin Features**: Admins can manage all content and users.

5. **UI/UX**: A clean, user-friendly interface.

1.2 Designing the Database Schema

Plan the database schema to define relationships between models:

- **Users**: Store user account details.

    o Attributes: email, password_digest, role (e.g., admin, regular user).

- **Posts**: Represent blog posts.

    o Attributes: title, content, user_id.

- **Comments**: Represent comments on posts.

    o Attributes: content, user_id, post_id.

1.3 Wireframing the Application

Create rough sketches of the user interface using tools like Figma, Sketch, or even pen and paper. Key pages to design include:

1. Home Page: Lists recent posts.

2. Post Page: Displays the post content and comments.

3. User Dashboard: Allows users to manage their posts.

4. Admin Dashboard: Provides admin controls.

---

2. Implementing Features

2.1 Setting Up the Rails Application

1. Create a new Rails application:

bash

```
rails new BlogPlatform --database=postgresql
cd BlogPlatform
```

2. Configure the database in config/database.yml:

yaml

```
default: &default
  adapter: postgresql
```

encoding: unicode

pool: 5

username: your_db_username

password: your_db_password

   3. Create and migrate the database:

bash

```
rails db:create db:migrate
```

2.2 User Authentication

Use the **Devise** gem for authentication.

   1. Add Devise to your Gemfile:

ruby

```
gem 'devise'
```

   2. Install Devise:

bash

```
bundle install
rails generate devise:install
```

3. Generate the User model:

bash

```
rails generate devise User
rails db:migrate
```

4. Add roles for admin users: Add a role column to the users table:

bash

```
rails generate migration AddRoleToUsers role:string
rails db:migrate
```

5. Update the User model:

ruby

```
class User < ApplicationRecord
  devise :database_authenticatable, :registerable,
    :recoverable, :rememberable, :validatable

  enum role: { user: 0, admin: 1 }
end
```

2.3 Posts

Generate the Post model:

bash

```
rails generate model Post title:string content:text
user:references
```

rails db:migrate

Set up relationships:

ruby

```
# app/models/user.rb
class User < ApplicationRecord
  has_many :posts, dependent: :destroy
end
```

```
# app/models/post.rb
class Post < ApplicationRecord
  belongs_to :user
  validates :title, :content, presence: true
```

```
end
```

Add controllers and views:

bash

```bash
rails generate controller Posts index show new create edit update destroy
```

Define actions in the PostsController:

ruby

```ruby
class PostsController < ApplicationController
  before_action :authenticate_user!, except: [:index, :show]
  before_action :set_post, only: [:show, :edit, :update, :destroy]

  def index
    @posts = Post.all
  end

  def show; end
```

```ruby
def new
  @post = current_user.posts.build
end


def create
  @post = current_user.posts.build(post_params)
  if @post.save
    redirect_to @post, notice: "Post created successfully."
  else
    render :new
  end
end


def edit; end


def update
  if @post.update(post_params)
    redirect_to @post, notice: "Post updated successfully."
  else
```

```ruby
      render :edit
    end
  end


  def destroy
   @post.destroy
    redirect_to posts_path, notice: "Post deleted successfully."
   end


   private


   def set_post
    @post = Post.find(params[:id])
   end


   def post_params
    params.require(:post).permit(:title, :content)
   end
  end
```

2.4 Comments

Generate the Comment model:

bash

```
rails generate model Comment content:text user:references post:references
```

```
rails db:migrate
```

Set up relationships:

ruby

```ruby
# app/models/comment.rb
class Comment < ApplicationRecord
  belongs_to :user
  belongs_to :post
  validates :content, presence: true
end
```

```ruby
# app/models/post.rb
class Post < ApplicationRecord
```

```ruby
  has_many :comments, dependent: :destroy
end
```

```ruby
# app/models/user.rb
class User < ApplicationRecord
  has_many :comments, dependent: :destroy
end
```

Add controllers and views:

bash

```bash
rails generate controller Comments create destroy
```

Define actions in the CommentsController:

ruby

```ruby
class CommentsController < ApplicationController
  before_action :authenticate_user!

  def create
    @post = Post.find(params[:post_id])
```

```ruby
    @comment =
@post.comments.build(comment_params)

    @comment.user = current_user

    if @comment.save

      redirect_to @post, notice: "Comment added
successfully."

    else

      redirect_to @post, alert: "Comment cannot be
empty."

    end

  end


  def destroy

    @comment = Comment.find(params[:id])

    @comment.destroy

    redirect_to @comment.post, notice: "Comment
deleted successfully."

  end


  private
```

```ruby
def comment_params

  params.require(:comment).permit(:content)

end

end
```

2.5 Admin Dashboard

Restrict admin functionality to specific users.

Add a before_action in ApplicationController:

ruby

```ruby
class ApplicationController < ActionController::Base

  def authenticate_admin!

    redirect_to root_path, alert: "Access denied!" unless current_user&.admin?

  end

end
```

Generate an AdminController:

bash

```bash
rails generate controller Admin index
```

Restrict admin routes:

ruby

```ruby
namespace :admin do
  resources :users, only: [:index, :destroy]
  resources :posts, only: [:index, :destroy]
end
```

3. Deploying the Project to Production

3.1 Preparing the Application

1. **Set Up PostgreSQL for Production**: Update config/database.yml for production:

yaml

```yaml
production:
  adapter: postgresql
  database: my_blog_production
```

username: <%= ENV['DB_USERNAME'] %>

password: <%= ENV['DB_PASSWORD'] %>

host: localhost

2. **Precompile Assets**:

bash

```
rails assets:precompile
```

3.2 Deploying to Heroku

1. Install the Heroku CLI:

bash

```
brew tap heroku/brew && brew install heroku
```

2. Create a new Heroku app:

bash

```
heroku create
```

3. Set up the database and push the code:

bash

```
heroku addons:create heroku-postgresql

git push heroku main

heroku run rails db:migrate
```

4. Open your app:

bash

```
heroku open
```

3.3 Configuring Custom Domains

Add a custom domain:

bash

```
heroku domains:add www.myblogplatform.com
```

Point your domain's DNS to Heroku.

---

4. Enhancements and Next Steps

1. **Add Pagination**: Use gems like **kaminari** to paginate posts and comments.

2. **Implement Search**: Add a search bar using **pg_search** or **Elasticsearch**.

3. **Add Categories and Tags**: Allow users to categorize and tag posts.

4. **Integrate ActionCable**: Enable real-time notifications for comments or likes.

In this chapter, we built a fully functional blog platform using Ruby on Rails. We:

1. Planned the app with wireframes and a database schema.

2. Implemented key features like user authentication, posts, comments, and admin functionality.

3. Deployed the application to production on Heroku.

By completing this project, you've gained hands-on experience with the core concepts of Rails development, deployment, and scalability. This foundation prepares you to tackle more complex applications with confidence.

Chapter 22: What's Next? Staying Current with Rails

The world of web development is dynamic, with new technologies, frameworks, and techniques emerging constantly. As you become proficient in Rails, the next step is to deepen your expertise by exploring advanced topics, staying updated with the latest developments in Rails and Ruby, and contributing to the vibrant open-source Rails community. This chapter will guide you on your journey toward mastery and long-term relevance as a Rails developer.

1. Exploring Advanced Topics: Hotwire and Turbo

Hotwire is a modern approach to building rich, interactive web applications with minimal JavaScript, leveraging Rails' existing strengths. It includes components like Turbo and Stimulus that integrate seamlessly into Rails.

1.1 What is Hotwire?

Hotwire (HTML Over The Wire) is a framework for building interactive web applications. Instead of using JavaScript-heavy front-end frameworks, Hotwire delivers fast, dynamic updates via server-rendered HTML.

1.2 Turbo: The Backbone of Hotwire

Turbo replaces traditional JavaScript frameworks with server-rendered HTML for many interactions.

Key Features of Turbo:

1. **Turbo Drive**: Replaces full-page reloads with fast navigation using partial updates. It intercepts link clicks and form submissions to enhance user experience.

Example:

html

```
<a href="/posts">Posts</a>
```

Turbo ensures the page updates dynamically without a full reload.

2. **Turbo Frames**: Enable partial updates to specific sections of the page.

Example:

html

```
<turbo-frame id="comments">

 <%= render @comments %>

</turbo-frame>
```

Only the comments frame updates when new comments are added.

3. **Turbo Streams**: Allow real-time updates to the DOM using WebSockets.

Example:

erb

```
<%= turbo_stream_from "posts" %>
```

Rails controllers can broadcast updates:

ruby

```
Turbo::StreamsChannel.broadcast_update_to
"posts", target: "post_1", content: render(partial:
"post", locals: { post: @post })
```

4. **Turbo Native**: Bridges the gap between web and mobile, enabling Rails views to power native mobile apps.

1.3 Stimulus: Adding Interactivity

Stimulus is a JavaScript framework designed for enhancing user interactions without overwhelming complexity.

Example:

html

```
<div data-controller="dropdown">
  <button data-action="click->dropdown#toggle">Toggle</button>
  <ul data-dropdown-target="menu" hidden>
    <li>Item 1</li>
    <li>Item 2</li>
  </ul>
</div>
```

Controller:

javascript

```
import { Controller } from "stimulus";

export default class extends Controller {
  static targets = ["menu"];

  toggle() {
    this.menuTarget.hidden =
!this.menuTarget.hidden;
  }
}
```

1.4 Why Adopt Hotwire and Turbo?

1. **Simplifies Development**: Eliminates the need for heavy JavaScript frameworks.

2. **Improves Performance**: Reduces client-side complexity and load times.

3. **Enhances Maintainability**: Keeps Rails at the center of your application's architecture.

2. Keeping Up with Updates in Rails and Ruby

The Rails ecosystem evolves rapidly. Staying updated with the latest releases ensures you leverage new features, improved performance, and security updates.

2.1 Tracking Rails and Ruby Releases

1. **Follow Official Channels**:

    o **Rails Blog**: weblog.rubyonrails.org

    o **Ruby Releases**: www.ruby-lang.org

2. **Subscribe to Newsletters**:

    o **Ruby Weekly**: A weekly digest of Ruby and Rails news.

    o **RailsConf Updates**: Insights from the annual Rails conference.

3. **Follow Key Contributors**: Prominent Rails contributors often share insights on social media and GitHub.

2.2 Adopting New Rails Features

When new Rails versions are released, they often include features that improve productivity and performance. Here's how to adopt them:

1. **Read Release Notes**: Release notes summarize changes and deprecated features. Start by reviewing them before upgrading.

2. **Test in a Staging Environment**: Use a staging environment to test the upgrade. Tools like **RSpec** or **Minitest** can catch breaking changes.

3. **Address Deprecations**: Run your application in verbose mode to identify and fix deprecations:

bash

```
rails server --verbose
```

4. **Upgrade Gems**: Ensure all third-party gems are compatible with the new Rails version:

bash

```
bundle update
```

2.3 Keeping Ruby Up-to-Date

Ruby releases bring performance improvements and syntax enhancements. Use tools like **RVM** or **rbenv** to manage Ruby versions.

1. **Install the Latest Ruby**:

bash

```
rbenv install 3.2.0
```

2. **Run Compatibility Tests**: Test your application with the new Ruby version using CI/CD pipelines.

2.4 Staying Current with Community Trends

1. **Join Local Meetups**: Participate in Ruby and Rails user groups to network and share knowledge.

2. **Attend Conferences**: Events like **RailsConf** and **RubyKaigi** are invaluable for staying informed.

3. **Engage in Forums**: Platforms like Stack Overflow and Reddit's r/ruby community provide answers to common questions.

3. Contributing to the Rails Open-Source Community

Contributing to open source strengthens your skills, builds your reputation, and gives back to the community that powers Rails.

3.1 Why Contribute?

1. **Learn by Doing**: Gain hands-on experience with real-world codebases.

2. **Build Your Network**: Connect with experienced developers.

3. **Enhance Your Resume**: Contributions to Rails or related gems showcase your expertise.

3.2 How to Start Contributing

1. **Find Issues**:

   o Start with issues labeled **good first issue** or **help wanted** on the Rails GitHub repository: github.com/rails/rails.

2. **Understand the Codebase**:

- o Clone the Rails repository and explore its structure:

bash

git clone https://github.com/rails/rails.git

cd rails

- o Read the contributing guidelines: Contributing to Rails.

3. **Fix Bugs**:
   - o Reproduce the issue locally.
   - o Write a test case that fails for the bug.
   - o Implement the fix and ensure the test passes.

4. **Submit a Pull Request**:
   - o Follow the project's pull request template.
   - o Provide clear descriptions and link to the relevant issue.

3.3 Contributing to Ruby Gems

Many Rails applications rely on Ruby gems.
Contributing to popular gems is another way to
make an impact.

1. **Identify a Gem**: Contribute to widely-used
   gems like **Devise, RSpec,** or **Sidekiq.**

2. **Improve Documentation**: Enhance README
   files or write tutorials for new users.

3. **Add Features**: Suggest and implement
   features that align with the gem's roadmap.

3.4 Creating Your Own Gem

1. **Why Create a Gem?**

   o Share reusable functionality with the
     community.

   o Solve problems others might face.

2. **Building a Gem:**

   o Use bundler to scaffold a new gem:

bash

```
bundle gem my_gem
```

- o Implement your feature in lib/my_gem.rb.

- o Publish your gem to RubyGems.org:

bash

```
gem push my_gem-0.1.0.gem
```

4. Best Practices for Staying Current

1. **Adopt Incremental Learning**: Focus on one advanced topic at a time, such as Hotwire or advanced testing.

2. **Engage with Mentors**: Seek guidance from senior developers to navigate complex topics.

3. **Invest in Professional Development**:

   - o Take advanced Rails courses on platforms like Pluralsight or Udemy.

   - o Read books like *The Rails 7 Way* or *Metaprogramming Ruby*.

4. **Stay Curious**: Experiment with adjacent technologies like **GraphQL, APIs**, or **Elasticsearch**.

Rails development doesn't stop at mastering the basics. To stay relevant and excel as a developer:

1. **Explore Advanced Topics**: Leverage Hotwire and Turbo to build modern, interactive applications.

2. **Keep Up with Updates**: Stay informed about Rails and Ruby's latest features and community trends.

3. **Contribute to Open Source**: Strengthen your skills and give back by contributing to Rails or related gems.

By embracing lifelong learning and engaging with the Rails community, you'll not only stay current but also become a valuable contributor to the future of web development.

Conclusion

As you've progressed through this book, you've embarked on a transformative journey into the world of Ruby on Rails development. From understanding the core concepts of Rails to building a functional blog application and diving into advanced topics like real-time features, security, scaling, and contributing to the community, you've built a foundation that empowers you to create scalable, maintainable, and impactful web applications.

This conclusion serves as a reflective summary of what you've learned, the value it brings to your journey as a developer, and how you can leverage this knowledge to continue growing. Rails is more than just a framework—it's a gateway to solving real-world problems through the art of web development.

What You've Accomplished

1. Mastering Rails Fundamentals

Rails is a developer-friendly framework, but its philosophy—centered on **Convention over Configuration** and **Don't Repeat Yourself (DRY)**—

requires an understanding of its conventions. Through early chapters, you've:

- Learned the **Model-View-Controller (MVC)** architecture, which forms the backbone of Rails applications.

- Explored the Rails routing system and how it maps requests to controllers and views.

- Mastered **Active Record**, Rails' powerful Object-Relational Mapping (ORM) layer, to interact with databases seamlessly.

- Built reusable and maintainable code through helper methods, partials, and layouts.

These core concepts are your first tools for crafting applications that are not only functional but also a joy to work with.

2. Building Real-World Applications

One of the most valuable aspects of learning Rails is applying its principles to real-world projects. The blog platform you built served as a comprehensive hands-on experience, helping you:

- Implement essential features like user authentication, CRUD operations, and commenting systems.

- Manage data relationships through associations like one-to-many and many-to-many.

- Integrate background jobs, caching, and other performance optimizations.

- Deploy your application to production, making it accessible to users around the world.

This project showcased the end-to-end development cycle and equipped you with the confidence to tackle increasingly complex applications.

---

3. Exploring Advanced Topics

Rails' versatility and depth allow developers to build not just traditional web applications but also modern, interactive experiences. Advanced topics such as:

- **Real-Time Features with ActionCable**: Leveraging WebSockets for live chat and notifications.

- **Hotwire and Turbo**: Simplifying dynamic front-end interactions without heavy JavaScript frameworks.

- **Scaling Applications**: Employing caching, load balancing, and containerization to handle high traffic.

- **Localization and Internationalization**: Adapting your applications for a global audience.

These topics enable you to transcend traditional application boundaries and deliver cutting-edge user experiences.

4. Security and Performance

Security and performance are integral to the long-term success of any application. Through chapters on these topics, you've:

- Protected your applications from common vulnerabilities like SQL injection, CSRF, and XSS.

- Secured sensitive data using HTTPS, secure headers, and encrypted credentials.

- Optimized application performance through query tuning, caching strategies, and background processing.

- Learned to scale applications vertically and horizontally to handle increasing user demands.

These skills not only ensure a robust application but also build trust with your users, who rely on the security and responsiveness of your platform.

---

5. Contributing to the Community

Rails is an open-source framework with a vibrant community. By contributing to Rails or related gems, you:

- Gain hands-on experience with collaborative development.

- Learn from experienced developers while improving the tools you use every day.

- Build your reputation and connect with a global network of like-minded professionals.

The Rails community thrives because of contributions from developers like you, who continue to share knowledge, ideas, and code.

Why Rails Matters

Despite the ever-evolving landscape of web development, Rails remains a relevant and valuable framework. Here's why:

1. **Productivity**: Rails' conventions reduce decision fatigue, allowing developers to

focus on solving problems rather than configuring boilerplate code.

2. **Maturity**: With over two decades of development, Rails offers a stable, feature-rich ecosystem trusted by startups and enterprises alike.

3. **Scalability**: Contrary to myths, Rails scales exceptionally well when combined with modern tools like Redis, Docker, and cloud platforms.

4. **Community Support**: The Rails community fosters learning and collaboration, ensuring that developers have access to resources, tutorials, and mentorship.

Rails empowers developers to build applications that range from prototypes to enterprise-grade systems with efficiency and elegance.

The Road Ahead

1. Deepen Your Expertise

Mastery is a journey, not a destination. As you advance, consider exploring specialized topics such as:

- **GraphQL with Rails**: Build flexible APIs that provide precise data to clients.

- **Service-Oriented Architectures (SOA)**: Break monolithic applications into smaller, maintainable services.

- **Microservices**: Build independent, deployable services for complex systems.

These advanced areas will prepare you for the unique challenges of large-scale applications.

---

2. Keep Learning

Web development evolves rapidly, and staying updated is key to remaining competitive. Here's how:

- **Experiment with New Features**: Each Rails and Ruby release introduces enhancements that can simplify your workflow.

- **Learn Adjacent Technologies**: Complement your Rails skills with knowledge of front-end frameworks (e.g., React or Vue.js) or back-end technologies (e.g., Node.js or Python).

- **Take Advanced Courses**: Platforms like Pluralsight, Coursera, or Udemy offer courses on advanced Rails and software architecture.

3. Contribute and Teach

Sharing your knowledge is one of the best ways to reinforce your learning. Start by:

- Writing blog posts or tutorials on platforms like Medium or Dev.to.

- Speaking at local meetups or conferences.

- Contributing to Rails or Ruby gems, helping others benefit from your experience.

4. Build a Portfolio of Applications

Expand your portfolio with applications that demonstrate diverse use cases:

- **E-Commerce Platform**: Implement complex features like inventory management and payment gateways.

- **Social Networking App**: Build user profiles, messaging systems, and activity feeds.

- **APIs and Mobile Backends**: Develop APIs for mobile apps or external integrations.

A strong portfolio not only showcases your skills but also serves as a repository of reusable code for future projects.

5. Engage with the Community

Join forums, Slack channels, or Reddit communities to stay connected with the Rails ecosystem. Events like **RailsConf** or local meetups provide opportunities to network and learn from others.

A Message for the Future

Rails development is as much an art as it is a science. The joy of seeing your ideas come to life on the web, knowing that you've created something impactful, is unmatched. Every application you build is a testament to your creativity, problem-solving ability, and dedication.

As you continue your journey:

- Embrace challenges—they are opportunities to grow.

- Stay curious—the best developers are lifelong learners.

- Collaborate and contribute—the community thrives on shared knowledge and collective effort.

The skills and knowledge you've gained through this book are just the beginning. With Rails, the possibilities are endless, and the tools are in your hands. Whether you're building applications that solve real-world problems, exploring cutting-edge technologies, or shaping the future of web development, remember that every line of code you write contributes to a larger narrative.

Welcome to the world of Rails—a world of innovation, collaboration, and endless potential. Your journey is just beginning, and the road ahead is filled with exciting opportunities. Keep building, keep learning, and keep creating. The web is yours to shape.